Student Study Guide

to Accompany

EXCEPTIONAL CHILDREN
An Introduction to Special Education

Sixth Edition

by

William L. Heward

Prepared by
Sheila R. Alber
and
April D. Miller

Merrill,
an imprint of Prentice Hall

Upper Saddle River, New Jersey   Columbus, Ohio

Editor: Ann Castel Davis
Developmental Editor: Linda Ashe Montgomery
Editorial Assistant: Pat Grogg
Production Editor: JoEllen Gohr
Design Coordinator: Diane C. Lorenzo
Cover Designer: Ceri Fitzgerald
Cover Photo: Shelley Gazin Photography
Production Manager: Pamela D. Bennett
Director of Marketing: Kevin Flanagan
Marketing Manager: Meghan Shepherd
Marketing Coordinator: Krista Groshong

© 2000 by Prentice-Hall, Inc.
Pearson Education
Upper Saddle River, New Jersey 07458

Printed in the United States of America

10 9 8 7 6 5 4 3 2 1

ISBN: 0-13-025749-4

Table of Contents

INTRODUCTION

TO THE STUDENT

We have prepared this guide to the sixth edition of Heward's *Exceptional Children: An Introduction to Special Education* with you, the student, in mind. This comprehensive review of your textbook's content should provide you with a useful resource for learning about exceptional children, their families, and the field of special education. You will discover that there is a great deal to learn about exceptional children and that mastery of this subject requires diligent study. Our goal is that this guide will contribute to your success in what we consider a very important topic—teaching exceptional children.

USING THIS GUIDE

This guide is divided into chapters corresponding to those in your text and each consists of six sections: Focus Questions, Chapter Overview, Chapter at a Glance, Guided Review, Objectives, and a Self-check Quiz. We have provide suggestions for using the various sections of the Student Study Guide's chapters to assist you in planning and organizing the use of this book and your own study routines.

FOCUS QUESTIONS

The Focus Questions address important issues from each of your text's chapters. You will find that the Focus Questions do not necessarily deal with specific details as much as they address larger issues and concepts that have general importance to a category of exceptionality or to the field of special education as a whole. You may find the Focus Questions useful as an introduction to your reading of a chapter or as a review of the chapter's content.

CHAPTER OVERVIEW

The Chapter Overview provides you with a brief summary of the content of each chapter. You may want to read the Chapter Overview after you have read its chapter as a means of review or as a means of introducing chapter content.

CHAPTER AT A GLANCE

The Chapter at a Glance features are a quick reference to the main topics, key points, key terms, and margin notes in each of the text's chapters. As with the Overview and Focus Questions, you may find the Glances useful as a review or an introduction to each chapter.

GUIDED REVIEW

Each Guided Review provides you with an opportunity to study in detail each of the chapters in the text. The Guided Reviews include a variety of questions to guide and focus your study of the important points in each chapter.

OBJECTIVES and SELF-CHECK QUIZ

Objectives are provided for each chapter to guide your study of the principal points. You may read the Objectives before reading each chapter to focus your study on the most important information. Each chapter in your study guide also concludes with a Self-check Quiz. An answer key is provided for each of the quizzes at the end of the study guide.

CHAPTER ONE
DEFINING SPECIAL EDUCATION

Focus Questions _____

- **When is special education needed? How do we know?**

Determining the need for special education is a complex and controversial task that is influenced largely by one's views of the purposes of special and general education programs. Basically, special education is needed when the physical attributes and/or learning abilities of students differ from the norm—either below or above—to such an extent that an individual educational program is required to meet their needs. How is the need for special education determined? The need is readily apparent for some students—their academic, physical, and/or social deficits or excesses are obvious. With other students, the need is not so obvious. Highly skilled and dedicated general education teachers working with other specialists and concerned parents are needed to identify students' needs and to provide specialized services.

- **If categorical labels do not tell us what and how to teach, why are they used so frequently?**

Some educators argue that a system of classifying children with exceptionalities is a prerequisite to providing the special programs these children require. Labeling allows special-interest groups to promote specific programs and spur legislative action, which ultimately makes more visible to the public the needs of exceptional children. In addition, labeling helps professionals communicate with one another, can influence education or treatment, and may lead to a protective response in which children are more accepting of the atypical behavior of the peer with disabilities. Other educators propose alternative approaches to classifying exceptional children that focus on educationally relevant variables, like the curriculum and skill areas that they need to learn.

- **Why have court cases and federal legislation been required to ensure that children with disabilities receive an appropriate education?**

Providing equal educational opportunities and services for children with disabilities closely parallels the struggle by minority groups to gain access to and enjoy the rights to which all Americans are entitled. An awareness of the barriers that have deprived these children of equal educational opportunity is important. Some people believe that special education is too expensive and that many children with exceptionalities cannot benefit from educational programming. Judicial and legislative action has been necessary to establish universal rights for children with disabilities. Our work as special educators is most often performed in local schools, but it is supported and guided by federal and state law.

- **Can a special educator provide all three kinds of intervention—*preventive*, *remedial*, and *compensatory*—on behalf of an individual child?**

Special educators can and do provide all three types of intervention for children with exceptionalities and their families. Preventive efforts are relatively new, and their effects will not likely be felt for many years. In the meantime, we must count on remedial and compensatory efforts to help people with disabilities achieve fuller and more independent lives.

- **What do you think are the three most important challenges facing special education today? Why? Read your answer again after finishing this book.**

This question is best answered by reviewing the current challenges presented in this and other chapters in the text. When responding to this question, consider local, state, and national perspectives—for each level of service delivery presents unique challenges. In addition, the attitudes and behavior of people without disabilities toward those with disabilities must be considered in meeting the challenges that face special education today.

Chapter Overview

Special education has "unlocked many doors" in the past several decades. The number of exceptional children receiving free and appropriate education has grown every year since a national count began in 1976, and much has been learned about how to effectively teach these children. The field has begun to identify and serve a new group of children, those who are labeled at-risk. Children at-risk are not disabled per se, but they are considered to have a greater than usual chance of developing a disabling condition. With many new preventive programs, more at-risk children are likely to be successful in the general education classrooms.

The four largest categories of children with disabilities receiving special education are learning disabilities, speech and language impairments, mental retardation, and emotional disturbance. The vast majority of children receiving special education have mild disabilities and approximately 75% of students with disabilities receive at least part of their education in regular classrooms.

Special education consists of purposeful intervention efforts at three different levels: preventive, remedial, and compensatory. It is individually planned, specialized, intensive, goal-directed instruction. When practiced most effectively and ethically, special education is also characterized by the use of research-based teaching methods and guided by direct and frequent measures of student performance. It is, however, a mistake to think that effective instruction for children with disabilities is distinctly different from effective instruction for nondisabled children. Good teaching is good teaching. The practices that contribute to effective instruction in the general education classroom also make the special education classroom a more effective learning environment.

A piece of landmark legislation, PL 94-142, the Education of the Handicapped Act (EHA) is discussed in detail. A long series of court cases has laid the groundwork for this law that forever changed the way that children are educated in this country. In addition, PL 94-142 has been amended three times and additional provisions and related legislation have been added. In 1990 the law was amended and the name was changed to "Individuals with Disabilities Education Act" (IDEA). The name remained the same, but the law was amended again in 1997. Other relevant legislation that has influenced special education is reviewed, such as Section 504 of the Rehabilitation Act which forbids discrimination in all federally funded programs on the basis of disability alone, and the Americans with Disabilities Act which extends civil rights protections to individuals with disabilities to private sector employment.

As a potential future educator, do not become overwhelmed by the current challenges facing the field. Special educators do not face these challenges alone; general education, other social and adult service agencies, and society, as a whole must help meet these challenges. If you choose to work with children with disabilities, most of your challenges will be more focused (e.g., teaching Matthew to read, helping Benjamin learn his math facts, teaching Erin to dress herself).

Although it is difficult to predict the future of special education, the best predictor of future performance is past performance; and the track record of the field is good. Special education has come a long way, and its future is promising.

CHAPTER ONE AT A GLANCE

MAIN TOPICS	KEY POINTS	KEY TERMS	MARGIN NOTES
Who Are Exceptional Children?	• Exceptional children are those whose physical attributes and/or learning abilities differ from the norm, either above or below, to such an extent that an individualized program of special education is indicated. • Disability refers to the reduced function or loss of a particular body part or organ. • Handicap refers to the problems a person with a disability or impairment encounters when interacting with the environment. • A child who is at risk is not currently identified as having a disability, but rather is considered to have a greater-than-usual chance of developing a disability if intervention is not provided.	• exceptional children • disability • handicap • at risk	• The word *handicap* is derived from "cap in hand" and conjures up the image of a person with disabilities begging in the street. *Handicapism* refers to the negative stereotyping and unequal and unjust treatment of people with disabilities. • Physicians also use the term *at risk* (or *high risk*) to identify pregnancies with a greater-than-normal probability of producing babies with disabilities. For example, a pregnancy may be considered high risk if the pregnant woman is above or below typical childbearing age, uses alcohol heavily, or is drug-dependent.
How Many Exceptional Children Are There?	• Children in special education represent approximately 10.6% of the school-age population. • The four largest categories of children with disabilities receiving special education are learning disabilities, speech and language impairments, mental retardation, and emotional disturbance. • The vast majority of children receiving special education have "mild disabilities." • Approximately 75% of students with disabilities receive at least part of their education in regular classrooms.		• What factors might be responsible for the huge increase in the number of children identified as learning disabled? Why has the number of children identified as mentally retarded decreased in recent years? Jot down your ideas and then compare them with what you learn later in Chapters 6 and 7.

Topic			
Why Do We Label and Classify Exceptional Children?	Some believe that disability labels can have a negative effect on the child and on others' perceptions of him or her and can lead to exclusion of exceptional children; others believe that labeling is a necessary first step to providing needed intervention and that labels are important for comparing and communicating about research findings. In curriculum-based assessment, students are assessed and classified relative to the degree to which they are learning specific curriculum content.	• self-fulfilling prophecy • curriculum-based assessment	• A protective response—whether by peers, parents, or teachers—toward a child with a disability can be a disadvantage if it creates learned helplessness and diminishes the labeled child's chances to develop independence (Weisz, 1981; Weisz, Bromfield, Vines, & Weiss, 1985). • Not all labels used to classify children with disabilities are considered equally negative or stigmatizing. One factor possibly contributing to the large number of children identified as learning disabled is that many parents view "learning disabilities" as a socially acceptable classification (Algozzine & Korinek, 1985; MacMillan, Gresham, Siperstein, & Bocian, 1996). Kauffman (1998b) contends that the issue of labeling is primarily a diversion and that our unwillingness to label children's behavior problems, especially young children who may be at risk for developing more serious problems, impedes prevention of more serious disabilities. • Children ages 3 to 9 can be identified as developmentally delayed and receive special services without the use of specific disability labels.
Profiles & Perspectives: What's in a Name? The Labels and Language of Special Education	The kinds of words that we use as labels, and even the order in which they are spoken or written, influence the degree to which a particular label serves as an appropriate generalized classification for communicating variables relevant to the design and delivery of educational and other human services. Everyone should speak, write, and think about exceptional children and adults in ways that respect each person's individuality and recognize strengths and abilities instead of focusing only on disabilities.		
Why Are Laws Governing the Education of Exceptional Children Necessary?	Prior to the 1970s, many states had laws permitting public schools to deny enrollment to children with disabilities. When local public schools began to accept a measure of responsibility for educating certain exceptional students, a philosophy of segregation prevailed.	• Brown v. Board of Education • Pennsylvania Association for Retarded Children v. Commonwealth of Pennsylvania (1972) • class action lawsuit	• Past practices were not entirely negative. Long before there was any legal requirement to do so, many children with special needs were educated by devoted parents and teachers. See Safford and Safford (1996) for an interesting historical account of educators' attempts to help children with disabilities over the last several centuries.

- Gonder (1997) provides enlightening profiles of several pioneering special educators and their students from the 1940s to the present.
- A *class-action lawsuit* is one made on behalf of a group of people. In the PARC case, the class of people was school-age children with mental retardation living in Pennsylvania.

- Special education was strongly influenced by the case of *Brown v. Board of Education* in 1954 in which the U.S. Supreme Court declared that education must be made available to all children on equal terms.
- In the class action lawsuit PARC (1972), the court ruled that all children with mental retardation were entitled to a free, appropriate education and that placements in regular classrooms and regular public schools were preferable to segregated settings.
- All children are now recognized to have the right to equal protection under the law, which has been interpreted to mean the right to a free public education in the least restrictive environment.
- All children and their parents have the right to due process under the law, which includes the rights to be notified of any decision affecting the child's educational placement, to have a hearing and present a defense, to see a written decision, and to appeal any decision.
- Court decisions have also established the rights of children with disabilities to fair assessment in their native language and to education at public expense, regardless of the school district's financial constraints.

The Individuals with Disabilities Education Act		
• The passage of IDEA by Congress in 1975 marked the culmination of the efforts of many educators, parents, and legislators to bring together in one comprehensive bill this country's laws regarding the education of children with disabilities. The law encompasses six major principles: • Zero Reject. Schools must educate all children with disabilities. This principle applies regardless of the nature or severity of the disability. • Nondiscriminatory Identification and Evaluation. Schools must use nonbiased, multifactored methods of evaluation to determine whether a child has a disability and, if so, whether special education is needed. • Free Appropriate Education. All children with disabilities shall receive a free, appropriate public education at public expense. An individualized education program (IEP) must be developed and implemented for each student with a disability. • Least Restrictive Environment (LRE). Students with disabilities must be educated with children without disabilities to the maximum extent appropriate and they should be removed to separate classes or schools only when the nature or severity of their disabilities is such that they cannot receive an appropriate education in a general education classroom.	• Individuals with Disabilities Education Act (IDEA) • child find system • free, appropriate public education (FAPE) • individualized education plan (IEP) • least restrictive environment (LRE) • Education of the Handicapped Act Amendments (PL 99-457) • individualized family services plan (IFSP) • related services • assistive technology • Armstrong v. Kline • Board of Education of the Hendrick Hudson Central School District v. Rowley • Irving Independent School District v. Tatro • Stuart v. Nappi • Honig v. Doe • IDEA amendments of 1997 (P.L. 105-17)	• Federal legislation is identified by a numerical system. P.L. 94-142, for example, was the 142nd bill passed by the 94th Congress. P.L. 94-142 was originally called the *Education for All Handicapped Children Act.* Since it became law in 1975, Congress has amended P.L. 94-142 four times, most recently in 1997. The 1990 amendments renamed the law *the Individuals with Disabilities Education Act*—often referred to by its acronym, IDEA. • Ann and Rud Turnbull (1998), who are special educators and parents of a young man with disabilities, describe due process as the legal technique that seeks to achieve fair treatment, accountability, and a new and more equal balance of power between professionals, who have traditionally wielded power, and families, who have thought they could not affect their children's education. • Chaikind et al. (1993) reported a per pupil annual cost of approximately $7,800 in 1989-90 dollars, or about 2.3 times the cost of educating each pupil in regular education. They found that costs of special education services varied considerably by disability category, ranging from under $1,000 per student with speech and language impairments to more than $30,000 per student with deaf-blindness. • Turnbull and Turnbull (1998) and Yell (1998) provide in-depth but very readable explanations of special education law and related court cases. • Browder, Lentz, Knoster, and Wilansky (1988) discuss the extended school year. • The Rowley case marked the first time a deaf attorney had ever argued a case before the U.S. Supreme Court.

- For a discussion of issues and considerations for disciplining students with disabilities in accordance with IDEA, see Katsiyannis and Maag (1998).
- The National School Boards Association (NSBA) defended the Rochester School Board when the district court's decision was appealed. The NSBA stated that local schools have no obligation to serve children on the "low end of the spectrum...because they have no capacity to benefit from special education."
- Table 1.3 summarizes key judicial decisions that have had significant impact on special education and the lives of individuals with disabilities.
- Table 1.4 summarizes federal legislation regarding the education and rights of individuals with disabilities.

- manifestation determination
- Timothy W. v. Rochester School District
- Gifted and Talented Children's Education Act of 1978
- Jacob K. Javits Gifted and Talented Student Education Act of 1988
- Section 504 of the Rehabilitation Act of 1973
- Americans with Disabilities Act (P.L. 101-336)

- Due Process Safeguards. Schools must provide due process safeguards to protect the rights of children with disabilities and their parents.
- Parent and Student Participation and Shared Decision Making. Schools must collaborate with parents and with students with disabilities in the design and implementation of special education services.
- IDEA requires states to provide special education services to all preschoolers ages 3 to 5 with disabilities. This law also makes available federal money to encourage states to develop early intervention programs for disabled and at-risk infants and toddlers from birth to age 2. Early intervention services must be coordinated by an individualized family services plan.
- Court cases have challenged the way particular school districts implement specific provisions of the IDEA. No trend has emerged, but rulings from the various cases have established the principle that each student with disabilities is entitled to a personalized program of instruction and related services that will enable him or her to benefit from an education in an integrated setting as possible.
- The Gifted and Talented Children's Education Act (PL 95-561) provides financial incentives to states for developing programs for gifted and talented students.
- Section 504 of the Rehabilitation Act forbids discrimination in all federally funded programs on the basis of disability alone.

	Key Terms	
		• Prevention can occur at three levels. *Primary prevention* consists of eliminating or counteracting risk factors so that a disability is never acquired. *Secondary prevention* is aimed at reducing or eliminating the effects of existing risk factors. *Tertiary prevention* involves the intervention with a child with a disability to minimize the impact of the condition. • Are there jobs in special education? Yes. There is a chronic annual shortage of about 29,000 certified special education teachers in the United States (Boe, Cook, Bobitt, & Terhanian, 1998) and 25,000 special education personnel other than classroom teachers (U.S. Department of Education, 1996). • The term *functional curriculum* is often used to describe the knowledge and skills needed by students with disabilities to achieve as much success and independence as they can in daily living, personal-social, school, community, and work settings. • Table 1.5 lists the definitions of six educational placements used by the U.S. Department of Education. • Where students with disabilities are educated— in particular, the extent to which they are included as meaningful participants in the instructional and social life of the regular classroom—is the most hotly debated issue in special education today.
	• primary prevention • secondary prevention • tertiary prevention • remediation • rehabilitation • functional curriculum • community-based instruction	
What Is Special Education? **Teaching & Learning in School: Signaling For Help**		• The Americans with Disabilities Act (PL 101-336) extends the civil rights protections for persons with disabilities to private sector employment, all public services, public accommodations, transportation, and telecommunications. • Special education consists of purposeful intervention efforts at three different levels: preventive, remedial, and compensatory. • Special education is individually planned, specialized, intensive, goal-directed instruction. When practiced most effectively and ethically, special education is also characterized by the use of research-based teaching methods, guided by direct and frequent measures of student performance. • Resource room teachers face a difficult challenge: the need to be in several places at once. Students in a resource room are usually working on the skills for which they need the most help. Students need an easy, quiet means of signaling for help, such as a signal flag, that allows them to keep working, with the assurance that their teacher will recognize their need for help.

	• For thoughtful analyses of contemporary specail education practice and the future of the field, see Kauffman (1998a) and Zigmond (1997).
Current and Future Challenges	Four major challenges that special education faces are: • bridging the research to practice gap. • making early intervention programs more widely available to infants, toddlers, and preschoolers who have disabilities or are at risk for developing a disability. • improving the ability of young adults with disabilities to make a successful transition from school to community life. • working more effectively with regular education to better serve the many students who have not been identified as disabled but who are not progressing in the general education program.
Profiles & Perspectives: Using the Internet to Learn About Special Education and the Council for Exceptional Children	• The Council for Exceptional Children (CEC), the largest special education organization in the world, has over 50,000 members including teachers, specialists, administrators, and parents of students with disabilities and gifted and talented students. Valuable information about a wide range of special education topics and issues can be found on CEC's website: http://www.cec.sped.org.

CHAPTER ONE
DEFINING SPECIAL EDUCATION

Guided Review

I. Who Are Exceptional Children?
    A. Exceptional children differ from the norm to such an extent that an individualized program of special education is required to meet their needs. The term *exceptional children* includes students who have/are:

        1. _____

        2. _____

        3. _____

    B. What is meant by the following terms?

        1. disability: _____

        2. handicap: _____

        3. at-risk: _____

II. How Many Exceptional Children Are There?
    A. Why is it impossible to state the precise number?

        1. _____

        2. _____

        3. _____

        4. _____

    B. How many children received special education services in the 1996-97 school year as reported by the U.S. Department of Education?

        1. _____ million

        2. _____ percent of the resident population

        3. _____ percent of the school-age population

C. Other numerical data on incidence of students with disabilities receiving special education services:

1. Since 1976-77, there has been a _____ percent increase.

2. _____ have been major contributors to the increase since _ 1986.

3. 91% of students are receiving services under which four disability categories?

   a) _____

   b) _____

   c) _____

   d) _____

4. How many states are serving students who are gifted and talented?

   a) _____

III. Why Do We Label and Classify Exceptional Children?
   A. What are the possible advantages of labeling?

   1. _____

   2. _____

   3. _____

   4. _____

   5. _____

   B. What are the possible disadvantages of labeling?

   1. _____

   2. _____

   3. _____

   4. _____

   5. _____

   6. _____

   7. _____

   8. _____

   9. _____

C. How does labeling affect eligibility for special education services?

1. _____

_____

D. What impact do labels have on instruction?

1. _____

2. _____

E. What is curriculum-based assessment?

1. _____

_____

IV. Why Are Laws Governing the Education of Exceptional Children Necessary?
   A. What practices have violated the rights of students with disabilities?

1. _____

2. _____

_____

3. _____

_____

4. What has recent legislation mandated?

a) _____

B. Separate Is Not Equal
   1. How was special education legislation influenced by the civil rights movement?

a) _____

_____

b) _____

_____

C. Equal Protection
   1. How did PARC v. Commonwealth of Pennsylvania influence special education legislation?

a) _____

b) _____

V. The Individuals with Disabilities Education Act
   A. What are the 6 major principles of the IDEA?

   1. _____

   2. _____

   3. _____

   4. _____

   5. _____

   6. _____

   B. What are the other provisions of IDEA?

   1. _____

      a) What is an IFSP?

         1) _____

   2. _____

      a) What are related services?

         1) _____

            _____

      h) What is assistive technology?

         1) _____

            _____

   3. What are the mandates concerning federal funding?

      a) _____

      b) _____

      c) _____

      d) What does IDEA stipulate about tuition reimbursement?

         1) _____

   C. What are the legal challenges to IDEA?
      1. What court case addressed an extended school year?

         a) _____

2. What court cases addressed related services?

    a) _____

    b) _____

3. What court cases addressed disciplining students with disabilities?

    a) _____

    b) _____

        1) What is manifestation determination?

           a. _____

               _____

4. What court case addressed the right to education?

    a) _____

D. Related Legislation
1. What federal legislation addressed the needs of gifted and talented children?

    a) _____

    b) _____

2. What are the provisions of Section 504 of the Rehabilitation Act of 1973?

    a) _____

       _____

    b) _____

       _____

    c) _____

3. The Americans with Disabilities Act (1990) extends civil rights protection of persons with disabilities to private sector employment, all public services, public accommodation, transportation, and telecommunications.

    a) How does ADA define a person with disabilities?

        1) _____

           _____

2) _____

_____

3) _____

_____

VI. What Is Special Education?
  A. Special Education as Intervention

  1. Preventive

  a) What are the three levels of prevention?

  1) _____

  2) _____

  3) _____

  2. Remedial

  a) What is the purpose of remedial programs?

  1) _____

  _____

  3. Compensatory

  a) What is compensatory intervention?

  1) _____

  _____

  B. Special Education as Instruction
    1. Identify the "who" of special education

  a) _____

  b) _____

  c) _____

  d) _____

    2. Identify the "what" of special education

  a) _____

3. Identify the "how" of special education

   a) _____

4. Identify the "where" of special education

   a) _____

C. Defining Features of Special Education
   1. What is special education at the level where exceptional children most meaningfully and frequently contact it?

      a) _____

         _____

VII. Current and Future Challenges.
   A. What four areas of special education are considered critical?

      1. _____

      2. _____

      3. _____

      4. _____

   B. What are other challenges in special education today?

      1. _____

      2. _____

      3. _____

      4. _____

      5. _____

      6. _____

CHAPTER ONE
DEFINING SPECIAL EDUCATION

Objectives _____

1. Define and provide examples for the following terms: *exceptional children*, *disability*, *handicap*, and *at risk*.

2. State the percentage of the school-age population receiving special education services, and name the four largest disability categories.

3. Explain the advantages and disadvantages of labeling.

4. Explain why laws governing the education of exceptional children are necessary.

5. List and describe the six major principles of the IDEA.

6. Describe the court cases which preceded the IDEA and the court cases which challenged the IDEA.

7. Define *special education* and describe the three levels of intervention efforts.

8. Explain the major challenges special education faces today.

Self-check Quiz _____

1. The term "exceptional children" refers to:
   a. children who perform below the norm academically to such an extent that special education services are required.
   b. children who receive special education services in separate classrooms.
   c. children who differ from the norm (either above or below) to such an extent that an individualized program is required to meet their needs.
   d. children who differ from the norm (either above or below), but do not necessarily require individualized special education services.

2. When a person's ability to function independently is limited only by his or her environment, this is referred to as a(n):
   a. impairment.
   b. handicap.
   c. disability.
   d. exceptionality.

3. Which population of exceptional learners is currently the most underserved?
   a. gifted and talented
   b. students with learning disabilities
   c. students with emotional or behavioral disorders
   d. students with physical disabilities or sensory impairments

4. Which of the following is NOT a benefit of labeling?
    a. Labels acquire the role of explanatory constructs.
    b. Labeling helps make the exceptional learner's needs more visible to the public.
    c. Funding is often based on specific categories of exceptionality.
    d. Labeling helps professionals communicate.

5. Approximately what percentage of the school-age population received special education services in the 1996-97 school year?
    a. 4%
    b. 8%
    c. 10%
    d. 15%

6. Under which disability category are most students receiving special education services?
    a. speech and language impairments
    b. mental retardation
    c. physical disabilities
    d. learning disabilities

7. Which case challenged a state law that denied public school education to children considered to be "unable to profit from public school education"?
    a. Brown v. Board of Education
    b. PARC v. Commonwealth of Pennsylvania
    c. Hendrik Hudson School District v. Rowley
    d. all of the above

8. Kyra was tested and placed in a special education classroom without her parents' knowledge or consent. Her school district did not comply with which mandate of IDEA?
    a. the right to a free appropriate education
    b. education in the student's least restrictive environment
    c. nondiscriminatory identification and evaluation
    d. due process safeguards

9. Even though Joshua, a fourth grader with a mild learning disability, could have profited from instruction in the regular classroom, he was placed in a self-contained special education classroom for 100% of the school day. Which IDEA mandate was violated?
    a. zero reject
    b. nondiscriminatory identification and evaluation
    c. education in the student's least restrictive environment
    d. none of the above

10. Physical therapy, occupational therapy, speech therapy, and counseling are examples of:
    a. related services.
    b. indirect services.
    c. assistive services.
    d. direct services.

11. Why is it impossible to state the precise number of people with disabilities?
    a. Different states employ different criteria qualifying students for special education services.
    b. Assessment procedures are imprecise.
    c. Some schools are capable of providing good prevention intervention.
    d. all of the above

12. Tyson, a student with learning disabilities, is functioning below grade level in reading. For one instructional period each day, Tyson goes to a resource room for intensive individualized reading instruction. Which of the following levels of intervention is Tyson receiving?
    a. preventive
    b. remedial
    c. compensatory
    d. all of the above

13. Which of the following is NOT one of the four largest disability categories?
    a. children with emotional and behavioral disorders
    b. children with speech and language disorders
    c. children with mental retardation
    d. children with physical disabilities

14. In a regular education classroom the curriculum is dictated by the school system; but in a special education placement, the curriculum is dictated by the:
    a. special education teacher.
    b. school psychologist.
    c. IEP team.
    d. collaborative efforts of the regular and special education teachers.

15. Knowledge of a child's disability category would enable the teacher to:
    a. pinpoint specific objectives to teach.
    b. oolect appropriate motivational strategies.
    c. determine the child's present levels of academic performance.
    d. none of the above

CHAPTER TWO
PLANNING AND PROVIDING SPECIAL EDUCATION SERVICES

Focus Questions

- **Why must the planning and provision of special education be so carefully sequenced and evaluated?**

  Federal law mandates a particular sequence of events that schools must follow when identifying and educating children with disabilities. This process is designed to answer a sequence of questions that makes both educational and common sense.

- **Why are collaboration and teaming so critical to the effectiveness of special education?**

  An appropriate education for students with disabilities can best be accomplished when both regular and special education teachers and other service providers work together to provide high-quality instruction for all children. The educational needs of exceptional children cannot be resolved by any single individual or professional discipline. Children with disabilities deserve the collective and collaborative efforts of all individuals charged with the responsibility of educating them.

- **What is an individualized education program, and how should its quality be judged?**

  The individualized education program (IEP) is the centerpiece of the special education process. IDEA requires that an IEP be developed and implemented for every student with disabilities between the ages of 3 and 21. The IEP is a system for spelling out where the child is, where he should be going, how he will get there, how long it will take, and how to tell when he has arrived. It is a measure of accountability for teachers and schools. Whether a school or educational program is effective will be judged, to some extent, by how well it helps children meet the goals and objectives in their IEPs.

- **Is the least restrictive environment always the regular classroom?**

  Judgments about the restrictiveness of a given setting must always be made in relation to the individual needs of the student. The regular classroom can promote or restrict a child's educational opportunities and skill development depending on the quality of the learning opportunities the child receives. No setting is, in and of itself, restrictive or nonrestrictive. It is the needs of the child and the degree to which a particular setting meets those needs which defines restrictiveness. Restrictiveness is a feature of place. But the physical place in which children receive their education will rarely be the only variable which determines the appropriateness of their educational opportunities.

- **Can high-quality, effective instruction be provided in any setting?**

  Yes. Keogh (1990) stated that "our greatest and most pressing challenge in the reform effort is to determine how to improve the quality of instruction at the classroom level." The learning and adjustment problems faced by students with disabilities are real, and their prevention and remediation require effective intervention. Regardless of who does it or where it takes place, good teaching must and can occur.

Chapter Overview _____

This chapter focuses on four general topics: the IEP (Individualized Education Program), the concept of least restrictive environment, teaming and collaboration, and special education reform. The passage of PL 94-142 ended the wholesale and often arbitrary exclusion of children with disabilities from the full range of experiences available in the public schools. Now we must address how to best meet the needs of exceptional children. Education is part of the answer, but answers to questions about the content and organization of that education will determine the direction and future of special education.

PL 94-142 requires that every child receiving special education services have a detailed written plan to guide those services and their delivery. This plan, called an individualized education program (IEP), is cooperatively developed by the school and the child's parents. Although an IEP is not legally binding, it is intended to establish a high degree of accountability for meeting the child's needs. As with many other aspects of special education, the practice of individual educational programming is not without controversy. Particular attention should be paid to what the IEP requires, why those factors are important, the special responsibility assumed by the schools, and due process rights afforded to parents. A student's IEP must specify where he or she will be educated. Children with mild to moderate disabilities far outnumber those whose disabilities are more severe. As a result, most children with disabilities are educated in regular school buildings and, increasingly, in regular classrooms. One aspect of the setting in which exceptional children are educated is its degree of restrictiveness.

There are two important points to keep in mind when evaluating the restrictiveness of a given setting: (1) the restrictiveness of a particular setting should be assessed in relation to the needs of the child, and (2) exceptional children, like all children, are all uniquely individual. An educational environment must support the academic and social behavior of the teacher, the regular education students, and students with disabilities. The teacher's obligation to teach and all students' opportunities to learn should not be dominated or controlled by any one individual or group.

The heart of PL 94-142 is the concept of appropriateness and the presumption that what constitutes an appropriate education for one student is not necessarily appropriate for another. Appropriateness cannot be decided solely on the basis of where a student receives his or her education, however. The how, what, and to what end of a child's education should be at least as important as the where.

Some students with mild disabilities require little more than alternative testing arrangements or minor modifications to the instructional design and presentation format traditionally provided in the general education classroom. It could be argued that if schools, in general, did a better job of addressing the needs of all learners, the need for special education would be eliminated for many students currently receiving special education services. For these students the issue of appropriateness with respect to the where of their education will receive little debate. The issue of how is usually easily resolved, and the issues of what and to what end are the same as for all other students in the elementary and secondary grades.

Other students with disabilities, however, present quite a different challenge to educational professionals. Considerations that focus only on the where of the student's education are likely to have only limited value for teaching the student functional skills and making long-term contributions to his or her prospects for independence. Similarly, focusing only on alternative means of teaching (the how) will also be of little value if the content (the what) provides the student with skills that have little or no application or utility beyond the walls of the classroom during that particular unit of instruction (the to what end). Both regular and special educators are responsible for insuring that the needs of exceptional children are met. Effective educational programs must be cooperatively and collaboratively planned and implemented. Individuals considering a career in education can expect to be involved in teaching exceptional children to some degree. Reforms that encourage the school to fit the student rather than have the student fit the school are likely to go a long way toward improving the education of all children.

CHAPTER TWO AT A GLANCE

MAIN TOPICS	KEY POINTS	KEY TERMS	MARGIN NOTES
The Process of Special Education	• IDEA mandates a particular sequence of events that schools must follow in identifying and educating children with disabilities. • Prereferral intervention is an informal, problem-solving process used by many schools to: (1) provide immediate instructional and/or behavior management assistance to the child and teacher, and (2) reduce the chances of identifying a child for special education who may not be disabled. • All children suspected of having a disability receive a nondiscriminatory multifactored evaluation (MFE) for determining eligibility for special education and to provide information about the child's educational needs and how to meet them. • An individualized education program (IEP) must be planned and provided for all children with a disability that is adversely affecting their educational performance.	• prereferral intervention • intervention assistance teams • evaluation team • multidisciplinary team • child study team	• Although not required to do so by IDEA, some states follow a process like the one shown in Figure 2.1 for planning individualized education programs for gifted and talented students. • Screening tests are relatively quick, inexpensive, and easy-to-administer assessments given to large groups of children to find out who might have a disability and need further testing. For example, most schools administer vision screening tests to all elementary children. • The evaluation team may not determine that a child has a disability if the primary factor for the determination is "lack of instruction in reading or math or limited English proficiency" [IDEA, Section 1414(b)(5)].
The Importance of Collaboration and Teaming	• Coordination, consultation, and teaming are three modes of collaboration that team members can use. • Three models for teaming are multidisciplinary, interdisciplinary, and transdisciplinary. Transdisciplinary teams conduct joint assessments, share information and expertise across disciplines, and select discipline-free goals and interventions.	• coordination • consultation • teaming • paraprofessional • interdisciplinary teams • transdisciplinary team	• *Paraprofessionals*—paid (and occasionally volunteer) workers who provide direct instructional and support services to students with disabilities under titles such as classroom aides and teacher assistants—are important members of many special education teams. Yet relatively little attention has been paid to their training and supervision (French & Pickett, 1997).

Teaching & Learning in School: Interactive Teaming	• Interactive teaming occurs when there is mutual or reciprocal effort among and between members of the team to meet the goal of providing the best possible education program for a student (Thomas, Correa, & Morsink, 1995). Skills needed for interactive teaming include interpersonal communication, role clarification, role release, and cultural competence.		• Regardless of the team model, team members must learn to put aside professional rivalries and work collaboratively for the benefit of the student.
Individualized Education Program	• An IEP planning team must include (1) the parents of the child; (2) at least one regular education teacher of the child; (3) at least one special education teacher; (4) a representative of the local education agency; (5) an individual who can interpret the instructional implications of evaluation results; (6) other individuals who have knowledge or special expertise regarding the child, including related service personnel as appropriate; and (7) the student, if age 14 or older, must be invited (younger students may attend if appropriate). • Beginning at age 14, IEPs must also include information on how the child's transition from school to adult life will be supported. • Without direct and ongoing monitoring of student progress toward IEP goals and objectives, the document's usefulness is limited. • The IEP is a measure of accountability for teachers and schools; however, a teacher and school cannot be prosecuted if the child does not achieve all of the goals set in the IEP.	• individualized education program (IEP) • IEP team • individualized family service plan (IFSP) • individualized transition plan (ITP)	• *Individualized family service plans (IFSP)* are developed for infants and toddlers (from birth until age 3) with disabilities. • Transition services are detailed in an *individualized transition plan (ITP)*, which becomes part of each student's IEP. • Over 55% of the 15,000 members surveyed by CEC's Division for Learning Disabilities reported that much of the paperwork required by the IDEA is unnecessary, duplicative, and costly (*DLD Times*, 1994). These teachers believed that excessive paperwork interfered with time available for providing services to students and contributed to some special education teachers leaving the field.

- Although the formats vary widely from school district to school district, each IEP must include these seven components: (1) the child's present levels of educational performance; (2) measurable annual goals, including benchmarks or short-term objectives; (3) the special education and related services and supplementary aids and services to be provided to the child; (4) an explanation of the extent, if any, to which the child will not participate with nondisabled children in the regular class; (5) any individual modifications in the administration of State or district-wide assessments of student achievement that are needed in order for the child to participate in such assessment (or alternative assessments); (6) the projected date for the beginning of the services and modifications described in paragraph 3 and the anticipated frequency, location, and duration of those services and modifications; and (7) how the child's progress toward the annual goals will be measured and how the child's parents will be regularly informed of their child's progress.

- All students with disabilities can and should be involved in the IEP process. The highest degree of involvement occurs when students participate as full team members and act as self-advocates.

Teaching & Learning in School: Someone's Missing: The Student as an Overlooked Participant in the IEP Process

Least Restrictive Environment	• The LRE is the setting closest to a regular school program that also meets the child's special educational needs. The LRE is a relative concept; the LRE for one child might be inappropriate for another. • The continuum of services is a range of placement and service options to meet the individual needs of students with disabilities. • The IEP team must determine the LRE after it has designed a program of special education and related services to meet the child's unique needs.	• least restrictive environment (LRE) • continuum of services • resource room • separate classroom • special school • residential facility	• Champagne (1993) has developed a sequence of steps that schools can use to make placement decisions consistent with the LRE requirements of IDEA.
Inclusive Education	• Inclusion (formerly mainstreaming) describes the process of integrating children with disabilities into regular schools and classes. • Studies have shown that well-planned, carefully conducted inclusion can be generally effective with students of all ages, types, and degrees of disability. • A few special educators believe that the LRE principle should give way to full inclusion, in which all students with disabilities are placed full-time in regular classrooms. • Most special educators and professional organizations, such as CEC, support inclusion as a program option but believe that the continuum of services and program options must be maintained and that placement decisions must be based on the student's individual educational needs.	• mainstreaming • inclusion • inclusive school	• Although often confused, the terms *inclusion* and *least restrictive environment* are not synonymous. Inclusion means educating students with disabilities in regular classrooms; the LRE principle requires students with disabilities be educated in settings as close to the regular class as possible in which an appropriate program can be provided and the child can make satisfactory educational progress.

25

Profiles & Perspectives: Inclusion Versus Full Inclusion	• Full inclusion is the most important and contentious issue in special education today. Inclusionists believe that the regular classroom's capacity to change is finite. Full inclusionists believe the primary job of educators is to help children with disabilities establish friendships with non-disabled persons and the placement of special-needs children in regular classrooms must be full-time.
Where Does Special Education Go From Here?	• The promise of a free, appropriate public education for all children with disabilities is an ambitious one, but substantial progress has been made toward fulfillment of that promise. • Implementation of the IDEA has brought problems of funding, inadequate teacher training, and opposition by some to integration of children with disabilities into regular classes. • Regardless of where services are delivered, the most crucial variable is the quality of instruction that each child receives.
Profiles & Perspectives: Moving Toward Inclusive Education	• We have moved beyond knowing whether inclusive education is viable, it has been demonstrated to be so for an ever widening array of students in increasing numbers of schools over many years. We need to continually remind ourselves that special education, namely, specially and individually designed instruction, is a portable service, not a place.

CHAPTER TWO
PLANNING AND PROVIDING SPECIAL EDUCATION SERVICES

Guided Review

I. The Process of Special Education
    A. How does a child who may need special education usually come to the attention of the schools?

        1. _____

        2. _____

    B. What are the purposes of prereferral intervention?

        1. _____

        2. _____

        3. What is an intervention assistance team?

            a) _____

                _____

        4. What is the role of the evaluation team?

            a) _____

II. The Importance of Collaboration and Teaming
    A. What is coordination?

        1. _____

            _____

    B. What is consultation?

        1. _____

            _____

    C. What is teaming?

        1. _____

            _____

D. What are three team models?

    1. _____

    2. _____

    3. _____

III. Individualized Education Program
    A. Who are the members of the IEP team?

    1. _____

    2. _____

    3. _____

    4. _____

    5. _____

    6. _____

    7. _____

    B. What are the seven components of the IEP?

    1. _____

    2. _____

    3. _____

    4. _____

    5. _____

    6. _____

    7. _____

    C. Beginning when the child is age 14, IEPs must include:

    1. _____

    _____

IV. Least Restrictive Environment
    A. To the maximum extent appropriate, children with disabilities will be educated:

    1. _____

    _____

B. What is meant by continuum of services?

    1. _____

    2. What are the seven placement options in the continuum of services?

        a) _____

        b) _____

        c) _____

        d) _____

        e) _____

        f) _____

        g) _____

V. Inclusive Education
   A. What is meant by inclusion?

    1. _____

    _____

   B. What does the research say about inclusion?

    1. _____

    _____

    _____

   C. Most special educators and professional organizations support inclusion, but believe:

    1. _____

    _____

VI. Where Does Special Education Go From Here?
   A. What types of problems has the implementation of IDEA brought about?

    1. _____

    2. _____

    3. _____

   B. What is the most crucial variable for successful special education?

    1. _____

CHAPTER TWO
PLANNING AND PROVIDING SPECIAL EDUCATION SERVICES

Objectives_____

1. Explain the purpose of prereferral intervention.

2. Explain the importance of collaboration and teaming.

3. Describe the three models for teaming: multidisciplinary, interdisciplinary, and transdisciplinary.

4. Identify the members of the IEP team.

5. List and describe the seven components that must be included on an IEP.

6. Explain what is meant by *least restrictive environment*.

7. Define *continuum of services*, and list the special education placement options from least to most restrictive.

8. Discuss the controversy of inclusive education.

Self-check Quiz _____

1. A child who may need special education usually comes to the attention of the schools because:
   a. a teacher or parent reports that the child may need special education.
   b. the results of a screening test may indicate a disability.
   c. the results of an IQ test may indicate a disability.
   d. both a & b

2. The purpose of a prereferral intervention is to:
   a. provide immediate instructional or behavior management assistance to the child and teacher.
   b. increase the likelihood of identifying a child for special education services.
   c. supplement a multifactored assessment.
   d. all of the above

3. What percentage of referrals lead to an evaluation for special education?
   a. 10%
   b. 50%
   c. 70%
   d. 90%

4. Assessment and evaluation for special education services are conducted by the:
   a. school psychologist.
   b. multidisciplinary team.
   c. special education teacher.
   d. IEP team.

5. The simplest form of collaboration in which ongoing communication and cooperation ensure that services are provided in a timely and systematic fashion is called:
   a. teaming.
   b. consultation.
   c. coordination.
   d. evaluation.

6. Which of the following teaming models is characterized by members of the team seeking to provide services in a uniform and integrated fashion by conducting joint assessments and sharing information across discipline boundaries?
   a. multidisciplinary teams
   b. interdisciplinary teams
   c. transdisciplinary teams
   d. child study teams

7. Which of the following teaming models allows team members to operate generally in isolation?
   a. multidisciplinary teams
   b. interdisciplinary teams
   c. transdisciplinary teams
   d. both a & b

8. Which of the following is NOT one of the suggested steps for interactive teaming?
   a. Designate a team leader.
   b. Decide which person will be responsible for delivering all services to the child.
   c. Describe the problem and allow team members to ask for clarification.
   d. Brainstorm possible interventions.

9. IDEA requires that an Individualized Education Program (IEP) be developed and implemented for every student:
   a. with disabilities between the ages of 3 and 21.
   b. with disabilities between the ages of 6 and 21.
   c. with disabilities from birth to age 21.
   d. with disabilities or at risk for developing disabilities between the ages of 6 and 21.

10. Which of the following components does NOT have to be included in the IEP?
    a. a statement of the child's disability category
    b. a statement of individual accommodations
    c. a statement of related services
    d. a statement of present levels of performance

11. IDEA states that specific IEP goals and objectives must be developed by the:
    a. special education teacher.
    b. special education teacher and the general education teacher.
    c. special education teacher and the parents.
    d. IEP team.

12. Which of the following statements is true?
    a. Students may not attend an IEP meeting prior to age 14.
    b. Prior to age 14, attendance and participation in an IEP meeting by the student is at the discretion of school personnel.
    c. Beginning at age 14, the student must be invited to attend and participate in the IEP meeting.
    d. none of the above

13. In the continuum of services, which of the following placement options is considered the least restrictive?
    a. regular classroom with supplementary instruction and services
    b. regular classroom with consultation to the teacher
    c. regular classroom and resource room
    d. full-time special class

14. "When presented with 20 multiplication problems of 2-digit numbers, Miyoko will compute the answers with 85% accuracy" is an example of a(n):
    a. annual goal statement.
    b. instructional objective.
    c. present level of performance.
    d. objective method of evaluation.

15. Most special educators and professional organizations, such as CEC:
    a. support inclusion as a service option, but believe the continuum of services must be maintained and placement decisions must be determined individually.
    b. believe that all students with disabilities should be placed in regular classrooms full time.
    c. believe that the continuum of services should be eliminated.
    d. believe that students with disabilities should not be placed in regular classrooms.

CHAPTER THREE
SPECIAL EDUCATION IN A CULTURALLY DIVERSE SOCIETY

Focus Questions

- **Why are culturally and linguistically diverse students disproportionately represented in special education?**

Culturally and linguistically diverse students are typically overrepresented in special education programs which serve students with disabilities, and underrepresented in programs serving gifted children. One possible reason for this disproportionate representation is the incongruence in interactions between teachers and culturally diverse students and families. Many expectations and values of the school setting may be incompatible with the expectations and values of the culturally diverse child's home setting. Teachers may interpret variations in behaviors and learning styles as disabilities instead of just differences. Another possible explanation for the disproportionate representation is the inaccuracy of the assessment and referral process. Figueroa (1989) calls the current practice of psychological testing of children from culturally diverse backgrounds as "random chaos" because it is so fraught with problems. Standardized assessments may discriminate against culturally diverse students by: using formats and items more relevant to one group than another, not taking into consideration the differing amounts of "test-wiseness," and assessing skills which may not be relevant to the skills demanded by culturally diverse students. Another factor which may lead to disproportionate placement of culturally diverse students in special education is the implementation of an ineffective curriculum and ineffective instructional practices.

- **What initial steps can a teacher take to become culturally responsive?**

While some would suggest that good teachers are born and not made, the multitude of skills required of highly skilled classroom professionals are acquired through experience over time. Culturally responsive assessment, curriculum, and instructional procedures will not become realities until teachers learn to appreciate diversity. The first step in becoming culturally responsive is to develop a general self-awareness and appreciation of diversity. This process begins with a thorough understanding, appreciation, and respect of the culture of others. Professional development through coursework, reading, and interactions with persons from cultural backgrounds different from one's own can all contribute to the education of diversity necessary for today's teachers. As with so many aspects of special education, teaming and collaboration are essential ingredients in developing attitudes and practices that are appropriately responsive to diversity.

- **What must educators realize and be sensitive to when attempting to involve culturally and linguistically diverse families in school activities?**

Teachers who are sensitive to and respectful of the cultural and linguistic diversity their students represent will have taken the first step in providing educational opportunities that are truly equitable. Because family involvement is so important to the success of children's achievement and school adjustment, teachers must make every effort to involve the families of culturally and linguistically diverse learners. When attempting to involve families of culturally diverse backgrounds, educators must realize that parents know their child better than anyone else does, may be intimidated by the educational system, tend to be family oriented, and have different experiences and views about disability. Taking these factors into consideration, teachers must approach family involvement with a great deal of patience, encouragement, and sensitivity.

- **How should assessment, curriculum, and instructional methods differ for students from culturally or linguistically different backgrounds?**

Stereotyping and discriminatory practices not only affect assessment results and instructional practices but also influence why a child is initially referred for special education services. Assessment protocols, curriculum decisions, and instructional practices that are not sensitive to the cultural and linguistic diversity present in a classroom can have a negative and lasting impact on children. Formal assessment instruments and curricular materials that have been developed for predominantly Caucasian, middle-class students are likely to give inaccurate results and require unrealistic experiential knowledge for children from culturally and linguistically diverse backgrounds. As with any culture, the family plays a central role in initial teaching and socialization of children. Educators must be sensitive to the needs of parents and family members from culturally and linguistically diverse backgrounds in planning individualized programs of instruction. Finally, while it would be a mistake to overgeneralize learning styles of particular cultural groups, knowledge about how different groups may respond to traditional teaching-learning situations will assist teachers' decision making and instructional design.

- **If a student cannot speak, read, or write English well enough to progress in the school curriculum, does it make any difference whether the limited English proficiency is caused by cultural differences or by a disability?**

Children with disabilities will experience difficulty learning in their native or dominant language as well as English. In answering this question, consider whether the child is only having difficulty learning English or whether the child has difficulty learning regardless of the language used. The teaching methods used in either case may be essentially the same, but the intent and philosophical basis of instruction will be different. Bilingual education is aimed at maximizing nondisabled children's academic development. Bilingual special education is aimed at maximizing exceptional children's achievement. This is a subtle but significant difference in educational focus.

Chapter Overview

Replace "diverse cultural or linguistic background" with "diverse reading or math skills," "diverse visual or hearing skills," "diverse motor skills," or any number of other descriptions that indicate that all children bring different skills and backgrounds to the classroom. With this point in mind, two issues are particularly important to the study of this chapter: (1) Every teacher must be responsive to the individual needs of every student and the unique personal and cultural history of each child that has contributed to shaping those needs; and (2) Fundamental principles of learning and effective instruction are applicable to all children; especially the extent to which children have opportunities to be successful in school and to be recognized for that success.

Acknowledging, understanding, and respecting cultural diversity is an essential attribute of every teacher. It is equally important to understand the potential impact that being educated in a system that serves a predominantly Caucasian, middle-class culture can have on the learning outcomes of children from culturally diverse children backgrounds. There is reason for concern because the achievement of culturally diverse children, as a group, is often below that of Caucasian children and a disproportionately large number of children identified as disabled come from culturally and linguistically diverse backgrounds.

Referral, assessment, placement, and instructional practices are all affected by the degree to which teachers and other education professionals respect and appreciate the unique needs of children from different cultural and linguistic backgrounds. An awareness of the cultural practices of specific culturally diverse groups such as African-Americans, Hispanic Americans, Asian Americans, Native Americans, and migrant students promotes teaching that is both effective and sensitive to students' culture. There is often a fine line between understanding and stereotypically assigning common characteristics to every member of a particular group. Just as all children with learning disabilities, mental retardation, hearing impairments, etc. are not the same, educators must not make the mistake of assuming that every member of a given cultural group shares the same attributes. All cultural groups are heterogeneous.

Discriminatory practices have and do occur in the assessment of children from culturally diverse backgrounds even though PL 94-142 requires that assessments conducted for the purpose of identifying and placing children with disabilities must be conducted in the child's native language. Most educational testes have been standardized on Caucasian, English-speaking, middle-class students, and even tests translated into a child's native language may be inappropriate for children from culturally and linguistically diverse backgrounds. A more meaningful method of assessment of academic and social behavior is to directly observe children not only in school settings but in their neighborhood and family settings as well.

Children from culturally or linguistically diverse backgrounds are not disabled by their linguistic and cultural histories. A child must be disabled in his or her native language for a true disability to exist. The goal of bilingual special education is not to teach children English. Its goal is to maximize the learning potential of students in the language they know best.

Respecting the cultural heritage of all students is one more factor to include in the mix of considerations for designing educational programs to meet the needs of exceptional students. All children bring a social, academic, and cultural background to class with them, and these backgrounds are part of the environment in which learning takes place.

CHAPTER THREE AT A GLANCE

MAIN TOPICS	KEY POINTS	KEY TERMS	MARGIN NOTES
Why Are There Disproportionate Placements of Culturally Diverse Students in Special Education?	• Although cultural diversity is a strength of our society, many students with disabilities still experience discrimination because of cultural, social class, or other differences from the majority. Educators must avoid stereotypes based on race or culture and become culturally responsive to differences in students from diverse backgrounds.	• culture • microculture	• The Division for Culturally and Linguistically Diverse Exceptional Learners (DDEL), a division of CEC, serves the interests of professionals working with culturally and linguistically diverse students with disabilities and their families.
Profiles & Perspectives: The So Called	• Students who are members of culturally diverse groups are typically underrepresented in gifted programs and overrepresented in special education. • Three factors may account for the disproportionate placement of students in special education: (a) incongruence in interactions between teachers and culturally diverse students and families, (b) inaccuracy of the assessment and referral process for culturally diverse students in special education, and (c) ineffective curriculum and instructional practices implemented for culturally diverse students.		• Pazcual Villaronga, a bilingual teacher in New York City's "El Barrio," reflects on his own culture in the poem "The So Called." He states, "The poem's energy is not so much out of anger, but rather more out of a burning desire to celebrate the many cultures within. And especially the ones that make me who I am!" (Villaronga, 1995, p. 260).
Becoming a Culturally Responsive Educator	• It is necessary for educators to become culturally self-aware prior to becoming responsive to students and families from diverse backgrounds. • Teacher education programs should include curriculum and field-based experiences related to teaching culturally diverse students.	• minority • culturally diverse	• "Never judge another man until you have walked a mile in his moccasins." This North American Indian proverb suggests the importance of understanding the cultural background and experiences of other persons rather than judging them by our own standards (Gollnick & Chinn, 1994, p.8).

36

<ul><li>The role religion plays in supporting families of children with disabilities has been documented by other researchers (Fewell, 1986; Haworth, Hill, & Gillen, 1996; Heller, Markwardt, Rowitz, & Farber, 1994; Rogers-Dulan, 1998; Weisner, Beizer, & Stolze, 1991).</li><li>Culture is only one influence on a family's reaction to having a child with a disability. Other influences, such as financial status, intactness of the family, external and internal support systems, and coping mechanisms, must also be considered (Correa, 1992; Harry, 1992a, b; Lynch & Hanson, 1998).</li></ul>	<ul><li>IDEA also requires that notice of IEP and placement meetings and other important conferences be given to parents in their native language.</li></ul>
Profiles & Perspectives: A Cultural Journey **Teaching & Learning in School: An Ethnic Feelings Book** <ul><li>Understanding family values and beliefs about education, disabilities, and school improvement of culturally diverse students informs teachers about their diverse students.</li><li>All of us have cultural, ethnic, and linguistic heritages that influence our current beliefs, values, and behaviors.</li><li>A project was designed to help students learn factual information about the historic experiences and contributions of their ethnic group by teaching cultural awareness units which involved students creating a feelings book that included factual information and students' interpretations of the feelings of their ancestors.</li></ul>**Appropriate Assessment of Culturally Diverse Students** **Profiles & Perspectives: Refugee Children from Vietnam: Adjusting to American Schools** <ul><li>Assessment of students for placement in special education should be fair; referral should be based on each child's needs, rather than on background.</li><li>Language plays a major role in the assessment of a student's educational and emotional needs.</li><li>Refugee children are a unique challenge for educators not only because they can be misdiagnosed, misclassified, or misunderstood but also because they may not receive appropriate services when they have disabling conditions.</li></ul>	

	• Siccone (1975) describes more than 75 multicultural activities to enhance self-worth, self-respect, and self-confidence in K–8 students. • The BUENO Center for Multicultural Education at the University of Colorado is an excellent source of materials and information for building cultural awareness in students with disabilities. • Figure 3.6 lists several specific strategies by which school staff can create a climate for promoting children's use of their first language (L1).
Culturally Responsive Curriculum and Instruction	• Multicultural approaches to curriculum include an equitable pedagogy that matches the student's learning style and the teacher's teaching styles and focus on providing an appropriate educational experience for all children regardless of their disability or ethnolinguistic background. • Cooperative learning has been an effective strategy for students from diverse backgrounds.
Thinking About Your Own Practice	• Skill diversity is another fundamental form of diversity in the classroom. • Regardless of their cultural background, all children benefit from good, systematic instruction. • The teacher must be sensitive, however, to the effect of cultural and language differences on a child's responsiveness to instruction.

CHAPTER THREE
SPECIAL EDUCATION IN A CULTURALLY DIVERSE SOCIETY

Guided Review

I. Why Are There Disproportionate Placements of Culturally Diverse Students in Special Education?

   A. What factors should lead us to be concerned about the role our education system has on the achievement of culturally diverse students?

      1. _____

         _____

      2. _____

      3. _____

         _____

   B. What 3 areas have been identified as integral to the disproportionate number of culturally diverse students in special education?

      1. _____

      2. _____

      3. _____

   C. What factors contribute to the incongruence between teachers and culturally diverse students?

      1. _____

         _____

      2. _____

      3. What is the definition of culture?

         a) _____

            _____

      4. What four characteristics of culture give us a background for considering the special needs of culturally diverse students (Gollnick & Chinn, 1998)?

         a) _____

b) _____

c) _____

d) _____

5. What is meant by heterogeneity within a culture?

a) _____

_____

6. What are microcultures?

a) _____

_____

7. How should diversity be defined?

a) _____

_____

8. How do tests discriminate against culturally diverse students (Brown, 1982)?

a) _____

b) _____

c) _____

9. Past overreliance on IQ tests has resulted in inappropriate placement. What are some examples of cultural bias in tests of cognitive ability (Hilliard, 1975)?

a) _____

b) _____

c) _____

D. Ineffective Curriculum and Instruction
   1. What factors may cause diverse students to lag behind expected benchmarks?

   a) _____

   b) _____

   2. Selected textbooks further accentuate the problems between traditional curriculum and culturally diverse learners.
      a) What are six forms of bias found in classroom materials (Gollnick & Chinn, 1998)?

      1) _____

2) _____

3) _____

4) _____

5) _____

6) _____

    b)   What is the ultimate goal of multicultural education?

        1) _____

            _____

    c)   To better meet the needs of diverse students, what three areas should be addressed?

        1) _____

            _____

        2) _____

            _____

        3) _____

II. Becoming a Culturally Responsive Educator
   A. Teacher Awareness and Development
      1. What is the first step to understanding and appreciating diversity?

        a) _____

      2. What is meant by self-awareness?

        a) _____

      3. What may educators do once they are aware of their own ethnic attitudes, behaviors, and perceptions?

        a) _____

        b) _____

      4. What are three methods for gathering information about cultures?

        a) _____

        b) _____

        c) _____

5. What concepts should teachers study to increase their understanding and appreciation of different cultures (Banks, 1994)?

   a) _____

   b) _____

   c) _____

   d) _____

   e) _____

   f) _____

   g) _____

   h) _____

   i) _____

6. Understanding verbal and nonverbal communication styles enhances:

   a) _____

7.. Understanding Multicultural Terminology
   a) What is meant by minority?

      1) _____

      2) Why is the term "minority" inappropriate?

         a. _____

         b. _____

   b) What is meant by culturally diverse?

      1) _____

B. Working with Culturally and Linguistically Diverse Families
   1. What is the influence of families on student success?

   a) _____

   2. The literature on culturally diverse families supports what six notions?

   a) _____

      _____

   b) _____

c) _____

_____

d) _____

e) _____

f) _____

III. Appropriate Assessment of Culturally Diverse Students
    A. What kind of assessment may be more appropriate for diverse students?

      1. _____

      2. What are examples of alternative assessment?

        a) _____

        b) _____

        c) _____

        d) _____

        e) _____

        f) _____

      3. What are four types of portfolios?

        a) _____

        b) _____

        c) _____

        d) _____

      4. Why should social and cultural background be considered when assessing performance?

        a) _____

_____

      5. How can examiners reduce the number of inappropriately placed students?

        a) _____

        b) _____

        c) _____

6. Attention to Language
   a) IDEA specifies the child must be assessed in his or her native language
      1) What serious flaw exists in the way this law can be implemented?

         a. _____

         _____

   b) Few reliable tests are available in languages other than English. What problems are posed by translation of English tests?

      1) _____

      2) _____

7. Avoiding Discrimination and Bias
   a) What actions should take place in the prereferral process to prevent unnecessary testing and inappropriate placement?

      1) _____

      2) What is the assessment and intervention model for the bilingual exceptional student?

         a. _____

IV. Culturally Responsive Curriculum and Instruction
   A. Culturally Responsive Pedagogy
      1. What are the characteristics of a culturally responsive pedagogy (Correa et al., 1995)?

         a) _____

         b) _____

         c) _____

         d) _____

   B. Bilingual Special Education
      1. What are the four approaches to bilingual special education?

         a) _____

         b) _____

         c) _____

         d) _____

2. What strategies should the teacher use to get his or her points across when working with LEP students (Briggs, 1991)?

a) _____

b) _____

c) _____

d) _____

e) _____

f) _____

g) _____

h) _____

i) _____

j) _____

k) _____

l) _____

m) _____

n) _____

V. Thinking About Your Own Practice
   A. How can teachers prevent inappropriate referral and placement of culturally diverse students?

   1. _____

   2. What are the characteristics of good systematic culturally responsive teaching?

   a) _____

   b) _____

   c) _____

   d) _____

   e) _____

   3. What practices should a teacher of culturally diverse students adopt?

   a) _____

CHAPTER THREE
SPECIAL EDUCATION IN A CULTURALLY DIVERSE SOCIETY

Objectives

1. Identify the prevalence of culturally diverse students placed in special education.

2. List and describe three factors that may account for disproportionate placements of culturally diverse students in special education.

3. Explain the steps teachers should take to become culturally responsive educators.

4. Describe appropriate assessment practices for students from culturally diverse backgrounds.

5. Describe strategies for designing and implementing a culturally responsive curriculum.

6. List and define the four approaches to bilingual special education.

7. Explain how teachers can implement culturally responsive instruction in their own practice.

Self-check Quiz

1. Which of the following statements is TRUE?
    a. The achievement of ethnically diverse students is similar to the achievement of Caucasian students in the early grades.
    b. The achievement of ethnically diverse students consistently lags behind the achievement of Caucasian students from preschool through high school.
    c. Ethnically diverse students drop out of school at the same rate as Caucasian students.
    d. The achievement of ethnically diverse students is similar to the achievement of Caucasian students until they reach high school.

2. Which of the following is NOT a contributing factor to the high percentage of culturally diverse students placed in special education?
    a. incongruent interactions between teachers and culturally diverse children
    b. inaccurate assessment of diverse learners
    c. ineffective instructional practices
    d. genetic predisposition toward acquiring disabilities

3. In Jeff's cultural upbringing, he was taught to convey attention and respect by avoiding eye contact with authority figures. Jeff's teacher, however, insists that he make eye contact with her when she is reprimanding him. Which of the following problems does this example illustrate?
    a. incongruent interactions between teachers and culturally diverse children
    b. inaccurate assessment of diverse learners
    c. ineffective curriculum and instructional practices
    d. context-embedded instruction

4. Rosa experiences more academic success in instructional activities which allow her to work with other students. However, her teacher usually requires all of the students in the class to work independently. Which of the following problems does this example illustrate?
   a. incongruent interactions between teachers and culturally diverse children
   b. inaccurate assessment of diverse learners
   c. ineffective curriculum and instructional practices
   d. context-embedded instruction

5. Which of the following is NOT a characteristic of culture?
   a. Cultural heritage is learned.
   b. Shared cultural customs bind people together as an identifiable group.
   c. Cultures have developed to accommodate certain environmental conditions.
   d. Culture is a static system that largely remains constant.

6. Which of the following statements about assessment is true?
   a. Standardized tests measure the extent to which diverse children have assimilated aspects of the mainstream culture.
   b. Testing methods used to identify children with disabilities are accurate and precise.
   c. IQ tests usually present a clear and complete measure of intelligence for culturally diverse students.
   d. Most children from diverse backgrounds have about the same amount of "test wiseness" as Caucasian, middle-class students.

7. Before teachers can implement culturally responsive curriculum and instruction, they must first:
   a. learn the language of linguistically diverse learners in their classrooms.
   b. develop self-awareness and appreciation of diversity.
   c. select instructional materials free of cultural bias.
   d. decide which values of culturally diverse learners are correct and incorrect.

8. Use of the term "minority" is inappropriate because:
   a. in some regions, culturally diverse people are the majority.
   b. the word "minority" carries negative connotations.
   c. using the word "minority" represents an attempt to categorize by race, not culture.
   d. all of the above

9. Use of the term "culturally diverse":
   a. is inappropriate because it has negative connotations.
   b. is inappropriate because it equates diversity with disability.
   c. is appropriate because it implies no judgment of a culture's value.
   d. is appropriate because it represents an attempt to categorize by race.

10. Which of the following statements about culturally diverse families is NOT true?
    a. Parents know their children better than anyone else.
    b. Most culturally diverse parents do not find the special education system intimidating.
    c. Many culturally diverse families have idiosyncratic ideologies and practices about the causes and treatment of disability.
    d. Culturally diverse people tend to be family-oriented.

11. Which of the following types of portfolios are used to inform the student and document self-reflection?
    a. showcase portfolios
    b. cumulative portfolios
    c. working portfolios
    d. student portfolios

12. Which of the following would be considered alternative assessment?
    a. observations and portfolios
    b. norm-referenced achievement tests
    c. standardized diagnostic tests
    d. IQ tests

13. Alternative, nonstandardized assessment methods:
    a. provide teachers with relevant and useful information about diverse learners.
    b. provide less accurate information than standardized tests.
    c. are not very useful for making appropriate instructional decisions.
    d. all of the above

14. When teachers use a hands-on approach to instruction, this is referred to as:
    a. context-embedded instruction.
    b. content-rich curriculum.
    c. interactive and experiential teaching.
    d. equitable pedagogy.

15. Juyoung, a 10-year-old Korean student, has been in the United States for 5 years. Her parents are concerned about her diminished use of the Korean language. Which of the following bilingual education approaches would enable Juyoung to regain her ancestral language?
    a. enrichment
    b. restoration
    c. maintenance
    d. transitional

CHAPTER FOUR
PARENTS AND FAMILIES OF CHILDREN WITH SPECIAL NEEDS

Focus Questions

- **What can a teacher learn from the parents and families of students with disabilities?**

For the vast majority of children, parents are their first teachers; and parents, for the most part, know their children best. It, therefore, would be short-sighted for educators not to develop productive parent-teacher partnerships. What teachers can learn from the parents and families of children with disabilities is as varied as the children themselves. Some parents will have a great deal to offer by providing a deeper understanding of the overall needs of their child, helping identify meaningful instructional objectives, encouraging extra practice of skills at home, and teaching their children new skills themselves. Other parents may be less involved in their child's education but can still provide important insight about the educational needs of their children.

- **How does a child with disabilities affect parenting?**

Evidence suggests that many parents of children with disabilities experience similar reactions and emotional responses and that most go through an adjustment process, trying to work through their feelings. Parents of a child with disabilities move from shock, denial, and disbelief to anger, guilt, depression, rejection, and overprotectiveness to, eventually, acceptance. However, parents and family members do not always move through the same stages in the same order or at the same time.

- **How can an educator who is not the parent of a child with a disability communicate effectively and meaningfully with parents of exceptional children?**

Educators who are not parents of a child with disabilities cannot know the 24-hour reality of being the parent of a child with disabilities or chronic illness. Nonetheless, they should strive for an awareness of how a child with special needs affects (and is affected by) the family system.

- **How might the nature or severity of a child's disability change the objectives of parental and family involvement?**

Parental involvement in any child's education is important. For parents of exceptional children, this involvement may be even more critical. Typically developing children acquire many functional skills without a great deal of direct instruction and deliberate practice (e.g., talking, playing, walking). The skills seem to come "naturally" to them. On the other hand, many children with disabilities will not acquire these same skills as easily or as independently as their "typical" peers. Their parents, therefore, must know how to directly and systematically teach these skills. The nature or severity of some children's disabilities also requires that their parents learn to use special equipment such as hearing aids, braces, wheelchairs, and adapted eating utensils. For many children with disabilities, acquiring, generalizing, and maintaining academic and social skills requires considerable deliberate practice of those skills. This additional practice is facilitated when parents and teachers work together.

- **How much parent and family involvement is enough?**

Kroth and Edge (1997) describe a model to guide parents involvement—The Mirror Model for Parental Involvement—that recognizes that parents have a great deal to offer, as well as a need to receive services from special educators. All parents should be expected to provide and obtain information, most parents will be active participants in IEP planning, and fewer parents will participate or contribute to workshops and extended parent education groups.

Chapter Overview

With most exceptional children come parents, families, or significant others. And most times that's fortunate. When teachers and families have effective partnerships a great deal can be accomplished for the exceptional child. This, however, has not always been the view of many educators. For years, some saw parents as either troublesome or uncaring. In recent years, the special education community has begun to recognize that a successful parent-teacher partnership provides benefits to the professionals, the parent and, most importantly, the child.

This chapter begins by examining the parent-teacher partnership. A productive parent-teacher relationship can provide teachers and other professionals with information and suggestions that benefit the child. A good working relationship with a parent can provide that parent with information and assistance for working with the child outside of the classroom. Perhaps most importantly, a productive parent-teacher partnership provides the child with greater consistency in his or her two most important environments, home and school.

Even though parents, families, and teachers consider a good working relationship important, it can be difficult to achieve. There are times when teachers and parents hold widely different opinions about what is best for the child. Some parents and teachers make false assumptions and hold negative attitudes about one another that causes antagonism and understanding of each other's roles and responsibilities. The chapter examines some of the barriers to effective parent-teacher relationships and identifies teacher behaviors that help break down these barriers.

During the last decade there has been increased involvement of parents in the education of exceptional children. Three groups of people have been primarily responsible: parents, educators, and legislators. More than any other group, parents themselves have been responsible for their increased involvement. They have formed effective organizations that have been the impetus for much educational reform. As individuals, they are learning more about the educational needs of their children and are seeing more potential benefits of an effective parent-teacher partnership. IDEA mandates that parents be involved in the planning of their child's educational program.

Parenting any child is a challenge. Parenting an exceptional child often comes with additional challenges. This chapter discusses the varied and demanding roles held by many parents of exceptional children. Do not, however, make the mistake of thinking that all parents of exceptional children react the same to their child's disability or have the same strengths or needs. Even though most parents of children with disabilities provide loving and nurturing homes, these children are overrepresented among reported cases of abuse and neglect.

Regular two-way communication with parents is the foundation of an effective parent-teacher partnership. This chapter briefly examines the three commonly used methods: conferences, written messages, and the telephone. Recommendations are included on how to prepare for and conduct more effective parent-teacher conferences.

Although educators' opinions vary on the role of "parent as teacher," there is compelling evidence to suggest that some parents can be successful teachers in their homes. It is important, however, for professionals to carefully examine to what extent parent tutoring is appropriate. Guidelines for parent-tutors, suggestions for planning and organizing parent education groups, and guidelines for working with parents are offered at the chapter's end.

CHAPTER FOUR AT A GLANCE

MAIN TOPICS	KEY POINTS	KEY TERMS	MARGIN NOTES
Support for Parent and Family Involvement	• Three factors are responsible for the increased emphasis on parent and family involvement in the education of children with disabilities: parent advocacy, educators' desire to increase their effectiveness, and legislators. • A successful parent-teacher partnership provides benefits for the professional, the parents, and the child.	• advocate	• An **advocate** is someone who speaks for or pleads the case of another.
Understanding Parents and Families of Children with Disabilities	• All parents and family members must adjust to the birth of a child with disabilities or the discovery that a child has a disability. This adjustment process is different for each parent, and educators should not make assumptions about an individual parent's stage of adjustment. • There are nine roles and responsibilities that parents of children with disabilities must fulfill: caregiver, provider, teacher, counselor, behavior management specialist, parent of siblings without disabilities, marriage partner, information specialist for significant other, and advocate for school and community services. • A family member's disability affects parents and siblings without disabilities in different ways during the different life-cycle stages.	• grief cycle	• Based on their observations of 130 participants in two parent support groups over a period of several years, Anderegg, Vergason, and Smith (1992) have developed a revised model of Blacher's work they call the *grief cycle*, which consists of three stages: confronting, adjusting, and adapting. • Respite care can reduce the mental and physical stress on parents and families created by the day-to-day responsibilities of caring for a child with disabilities. • George (1988) describes a group support program designed to help grandparents and extended family members of children with disabilities develop positive and supportive roles that help the child and the parents.

		- The strategies recommended in this section are relevant to all types of parent-teacher meetings. However, IEP and IFSP planning and evaluation meetings, which are discussed in Chapters 2 and 5 respectively, entail additional procedural requirements. - Teachers should never rely on written messages, regardless of their form, as the sole method of communicating with parents. Teachers must also be sensitive to the cultural and linguistic backgrounds and educational levels of parents. For example, Harry (1992a) reports that because one group of Hispanic parents had to spend a great deal of time translating and trying to understand a school's written messages, they viewed those messages as a nuisance that further alienated them from their children's school. - Telephone trees can be an efficient way to get information to all parents associated with a class. The teacher calls two or three parents, each of whom calls two or three more, and so on. A telephone tree gets parents actively involved and gives them an opportunity to get to know one another.
Profiles & Perspectives: Abuse and Neglect of Children with Disabilities	- Respite care—the temporary care of an individual with disabilities by nonfamily members—is a critical support for families with children with severe disabilities. - Children with disabilities are overrepresented among reported cases of child abuse and neglect. Most parents of children with disabilities provided a loving and supportive home.	
Parent-Teacher Communication	- Regular two-way communication is critical to parent-teacher partnerships. - Conferences, written messages, and telephone calls are three ways to maintain communication. - Do not assume you know more about a child than do the parents. - Speak in plain, everyday language. - Do not use generalizations or assumptions. - Be sensitive and responsive to cultural and linguistic differences. - Do not be defensive toward or intimidated by parents. - Keep concern for the child at the forefront. - Help parents strive for realistic optimism. - Start with something with which parents can be successful. - Do not be afraid to say, "I don't know."	

- Ammer and Littleton (1983) asked 217 parents of exceptional children to check which methods they preferred for receiving regular information from school. Letters were the most popular, checked by 69% of parents. The next most popular were parent-teacher conferences (51%) and telephone calls from teachers (45%). Home visits (19%) were the least preferred method of establishing or improving home-school communication.

- Cone, Delawyer, and Wolfe (1985) developed the parent/family involvement index to objectively measure 12 types of parent involvement in a special education program.

- positive behavioral support
- functional assessment
- open needs assessment
- closed needs assessment

Other Types of Parent Involvement

- Many parents can and should learn to help teach their child with disabilities.
- Parents and professionals should work together in planning and conducting parent education groups.
- Parent to Parent groups give parents of children with disabilities support from veteran parents who are experiencing similar circumstances and challenges.
- Parents who serve as action research partners help brainstorm research questions, collect performance data on their children, and share those data with other parents and teachers.
- The mirror model of parent involvement assumes that not all parents need everything professionals have to offer and should not be expected to participate in everything.

Teaching & Learning in School: A Parent-Professional Partnership in Positive Behavioral Support

- Using positive behavioral supports and functional assessments resulted in virtually eliminating severe behaviors and decreasing the family members' reprimands for a young boy with disabilities.

	• family supports • strength-based approach	• Dunlap and Fox (1997) define **family supports** as "any and all actions that serve to strengthen and sustain the family system, especially as these actions pertain to the family's assimilation and understanding of the child's disability" (p.4).
Profiles & Perspectives: In Support of Jay		• Perspectives from a parent and teacher using different forms of communication (in-service program, home-school notebook, parent-teacher conferences, inventories). Continued communication with the family is critical to the success of any school program.
Current Issues and Future Trends		• Professionals who work with parents should value family needs and support families in maintaining control over the services and supports they receive. • The rationale for family empowerment is based on the belief that families are the primary and most effective social institution, families cannot be replaced, parents are and should remain in charge of their families, and the role of professionals is to help parents in their capacity as family leaders. • Family-centered services are predicated on the belief that the child is part of a family system and that effective change for the child cannot be achieved without helping the entire family. • A strength-based approach to family supports assumes that all families have strengths they can build on and use to meet their own needs, accomplish their own goals, and promote the well-being of family members.

CHAPTER FOUR
PARENTS AND FAMILIES OF CHILDREN WITH SPECIAL NEEDS

Guided Review

I. Support for Parent and Family Involvement
    A. What factors contribute to an increased emphasis and need for greater collaboration between parents and teachers?

    1. _____

    2. _____

    3. _____

    B. Parents Advocate for Change
       1. What primary role do parents play in bringing about equal access to educational opportunities for their children?

       a) _____

       2. What four powerful arguments view active family involvement as the "cornerstone of relevant and longitudinal educational planning"?

       a) _____

       _____

       b) _____

       _____

       c) _____

       _____

       d) _____

       _____

    C. Educators Strive for Greater Effectiveness and Significance
       1. What expanded role beyond the three Rs does classroom teaching now require to ensure successful functioning of students with disabilities?

       a) _____

       b) _____

c) _____

d) _____

2. Why do teachers need to look to parents and families for assistance in planning and designing instructional programs for students with disabilities?

a) _____

_____

b) _____

c) _____

d) _____

_____

D. Legislators Mandate Parent and Family Participation
1. In what six areas do the 1997 statutory guidelines of the reauthorization of IDEA indicate schools must work closely with parents of children with disabilities?

a) _____

b) _____

c) _____

d) _____

e) _____

f) _____

2. If parents believe their needs are not being met, what recourse do they have according to the 1997 IDEA?

a) _____

3. What additional three factors are most important to developing a relationship with parents and families of children with disabilities?

a) _____

_____

b) _____

c) _____

II. Understanding Parents and Families of Children with Disabilities
  A. Impact of a Child with Disabilities on the Family
    1. What three typical stages do parents go through in adjusting to the birth of a child with disabilities?

       a) _____

          _____

       b) _____

          _____

       c) _____

    2. What stage beyond acceptance do many families of children with disabilities reach and what evidences this stage?

       a) _____

          _____

       b) _____

       c) _____

    3. Even though parents and families experience different sequences and experiences in adjusting to life with a child with disabilities, what common thread can make adjustment easier?

       a) _____

  B. The Many Roles of an Exceptional Parent
    1. What various roles might a parent of a child with disabilities have to play and how might that responsibility differ from the roles of a parent or the family of a typical child?

       a) _____

          _____

       b) _____

          _____

       c) _____

          _____

       d) _____

          _____

       e) _____

          _____

f) _____

_____

g) _____

_____

h) _____

_____

i) _____

_____

C. Changing Needs as Children Grow
1. What typical issues might parents or siblings need to address during the four life-cycle _
changes children with disabilities undergo?
a) early childhood:

1) _____

2) _____

b) childhood:

1) _____

2) _____

c) adolescence:

1) _____

2) _____

d) adulthood:

1) _____

2) _____

III. Parent-Teacher Communication
A. What are five principles of effective communication?

1. _____

2. _____

3. _____

4. _____

5. _____

B. What are the basic barriers to effective parent-teacher communication?

   1. _____

   2. _____

   3. _____

C. Methods of Home-School Communication
   1. Parent-Teacher Conferences
      a) How can teachers effectively prepare the conference?

         1) _____

         2) _____

         3) _____

      b) Why are conferences usually held in the child's classroom?

         1) _____

         2) _____

         3) _____

         4) _____

      c) What is the four-step sequence for parent-teacher conferences?

         1) _____

         2) _____

         3) _____

         4) _____

   2. What are the different types of written message systems?

      a) _____

      b) _____

      c) _____

      d) _____

      e) _____

3. How can telephone calls be used to maintain effective and efficient communication?

   a) _____

   _____

   b) _____

   _____

   c) _____

   _____

   d) _____

   e) _____

4. How can the answering machine be used for home-school communication?

   a) _____

   _____

IV. Other Types of Parent Involvement
   A. Parents as Teachers
      1. What are five guidelines for home-based parent tutoring?

         a) _____

         b) _____

         c) _____

         d) _____

         e) _____

   B. Parent Education and Support Groups
      1. What purposes are parent groups designed to accomplish?

         a) _____

         b) _____

         c) _____

      2. What is an open needs assessment?

         a) _____

3. What is a closed needs assessment?

    a) _____

C. What is the purpose of a Parent to Parent group?

    1. _____

D. Parents as Research Partners. What steps are recommended for parent participation in action research?

    1. _____

    2. _____

    3. _____

    4. _____

    5. _____

    6. _____

    7. _____

    8. _____

E. How Much Parent Involvement?
    1. What is the mirror model for parent involvement?

        a) _____

           _____

           _____

V. Current Issues and Future Trends
    A. What values are suggested by the Syracuse University Center on Human Policy (1997)?

        1. _____

           _____

        2. _____

           _____

        3. _____

           _____

B. The rationale for family empowerment is based on what beliefs?

1. _____

2. _____

3. _____

4. _____

C. What is a strength-based approach?

1. _____

_____

_____

CHAPTER FOUR
PARENTS AND FAMILIES OF CHILDREN WITH SPECIAL NEEDS

Objectives

1. Explain the factors responsible for increased parental and family involvement in the education of children with disabilities.

2. Describe the benefits of a successful parent-teacher partnership.

3. Explain the roles and responsibilities of parents who have children with disabilities.

4. Define *respite care*.

5. Explain the five principles of effective communication between educators and parents.

6. Describe the most common modes of home-school communication.

7. Describe the guidelines for working with parents and families of children with disabilities.

8. Explain the mirror model of parent involvement.

9. Discuss the concept of family-centered services.

10. Explain what is meant by a strength-based approach to family supports.

Self-check Quiz

1. Which of the following is NOT a contributing factor to the increased emphasis on collaboration between parents and teachers in the education of exceptional children?
   a. Parents want to be involved.
   b. Educational effectiveness is enhanced when parents are involved.
   c. The law requires collaboration.
   d. none of the above

2. How does a child with disabilities benefit from a working relationship between parents and educators?
   a. The child receives more support from home and less support from school.
   b. The child has access to expanded resources and services.
   c. The child receives increased opportunities for social interaction with peers.
   d. both a & b

3. Which of the following is NOT one of the stages of adjustment identified by Blacher (1984)?
    a. denial
    b. emotional disorganization
    c. bargaining
    d. acceptance

4. Which of the following statements is true regarding parents' adjustment to having a child with disabilities?
    a. The sequence and time needed for adjustment are the same for all parents.
    b. The stages of adjustment should not be emphasized as a basis for planning family services.
    c. Parents who do not progress through the stages of adjustment within a reasonable amount of time are most likely to have a mental illness due to stress.
    d. both b & c

5. Families of children with disabilities tend to experience higher levels of stress at which stage in the child's life cycle?
    a. early childhood
    b. elementary school age
    c. adolescence
    d. all stages of childhood are equally stressful

6. Most parents of young children with developmental disabilities are mainly concerned about:
    a. having a family life.
    b. monetary concerns.
    c. how the child with developmental disabilities appears to their peers.
    d. medical and health problems.

7. The number of children who are victims of child abuse and neglect has:
    a. remained the same since 1990.
    b. increased by about 8% since 1990.
    c. increased by about 18% since 1990.
    d. decreased by about 3% since 1990.

8. Which of the following statements is true?
    a. Children with and without disabilities are equally likely to be abused or neglected.
    b. Children with disabilities are more likely to be abused or neglected for longer periods of time than children without disabilities.
    c. Children with disabilities are less likely to be abused than children without disabilities.
    d. both a & b

9. In order for the home-school dialogue notebooks system of communication to work, parent responses are vital. How can teachers encourage parent participation in communication?
    a. by being organized and persistent
    b. by rewarding the student with extra privileges when parents sign the notebook
    c. by using the notebook as a part of the child's grade
    d. all of the above

10. Which of the following teachers is demonstrating an effective principle of communication?
    a. Mr. Roth engages in extended small talk with parents in order to maintain rapport.
    b. In order to stay focused, Ms. Felini avoids open-ended questions.
    c. Ms. Bellamy makes a positive comment before and after she tells the parents about a problem.
    d. Mr. Kuzinski encourages parents to speak freely by acting like he agrees with everything they say.

11. Parents are more likely to carry out teaching tasks that:
    a. are part of the daily routine.
    b. require only about 20 to 25 minutes each.
    c. also occur frequently at school.
    d. both a & b

12. A parent asks how she can make the tutoring session with her child more effective. Which of the following statements should the teacher offer as advice to the parent?
    a. Provide unemotional responses to their child's errors.
    b. Keep a record of each session.
    c. To ensure maximum effectiveness, each tutoring session should be at least 30 to 40 minutes.
    d. both a & b

13. The mirror model for parent involvement assumes that:
    a. parents have information, knowledge, and skills that are of little use to professionals for developing appropriate instruction.
    b. the skills the professional demonstrates at school with the child should be reflected in the home by the parent.
    c. no parent should be expected to participate in everything and not all parents need everything a professional has to offer.
    d. none of the above

14. When using the strength-based approach to family supports, a professional should:
    a. start with an assessment of problems related to the child with disabilities.
    b. attempt to fully understand the way a family accomplishes its goals.
    c. conduct a formal needs assessment.
    d. all of the above

15. What are the most common methods of communication between teachers and parents?
    a. written messages and telephone calls
    b. parent-teacher conferences, written messages, and telephone calls
    c. written messages and parent-teacher conferences
    d. phone calls and parent-teacher conferences

CHAPTER FIVE
EARLY CHILDHOOD SPECIAL EDUCATION

Focus Questions

- **Why is it so difficult to measure the impact of early intervention?**

The main goal of early intervention programs is to lessen the detrimental effects of some present risk factor on a child's later development. Measures of the effectiveness of an early intervention program entail a number of considerations at different points in time. It is difficult to judge the overall effectiveness of early intervention programs. For example, can we know for certain whether an early intervention program was responsible for a child's needing only occasional tutoring rather than a full-time special education placement? Or can we credit or blame early intervention efforts when a child did not require special education until fourth grade rather than first grade? There are many factors that influence the extent to which a treatment is effective. This is particularly true when the goal of the treatment is preventive, as it is with early intervention programs.

- **How can we provide early intervention services for a child whose disability is not yet present?**

A child who has been identified as being at risk for developing a disability because of environmental or biological factors should receive preventive programming before any evidence of a disability exists. Parents and teachers do not have to wait until a delay in development occurs before they begin to interact with their children in ways that promote learning and development. Similarly, medical professionals do not need to wait and observe health or biological conditions before they can prescribe various precautionary or preventive procedures for the family to follow on behalf of the child. Intervention programs can never be started too early. Every reasonable precautionary and preventive measure that can be taken to ensure that the child does not develop a disability should be pursued.

- **What are the goals of early childhood special education? Which do you think are most important?**

The goals of early childhood special education are: (a) support families in achieving their own goals; (b) promote child engagement, independence, and mastery; (c) promote development in all important domains; (d) build and support social competence; (e) facilitate the generalized use of skills; (f) prepare and assist children for normalized life experiences with their families, in school, and in their communities; (g) help children and their families make smooth transitions; and (h) prevent or minimize the development of future problems or disabilities. After studying the goals, you should recognize that many are interrelated and all are intended to lead to increased independence and competency of individual children. All of the goals address the child within the context of the family and the community. Pay particular attention to the last one, "prevent or minimize the development of future problems or disabilities." This goal can only be accomplished if the other seven are also the focus of early education efforts for children with special needs.

- **In what ways might a program based entirely on developmentally appropriate practices not always be sufficient for a young child with disabilities?**

A developmentally based curriculum is intended to accelerate development progress. Why, then, wouldn't a development curriculum always make sense for a child who is behind in development? If, for example, a four-year-old is unable to feed himself, a developmental approach might focus on prerequisite skills to self-feeding such as eye-hand coordination, fine motor skills, and body position in space. None of these prerequisites, however, translates directly into self-feeding. In addition, not every developmental milestone is equivalent to a functional skill for the child. For many children with developmental delays, the goal is not a matter of development on a par with nondisabled peers but of gaining useful skills that will contribute to independence. Self-feeding is an essential part of independent living. A functionally-based curriculum directly teaches those skills that will increase the child's level of independence. In other words, our four-year-old will be taught to use a spoon, plate, and cup so that he can eat with minimum assistance and maximum independence.

- **How can a play activity or everyday routine be turned into a specially designed learning opportunity for a child with disabilities?**

  Teaching when skills would normally happen increases the likelihood of generalization and maintenance because it " duplicates the occasions in which the skill should occur after instruction ceases."

Chapter Overview

Early intervention is often proactive rather than reactive. Prenatal care and parental education can reduce or sometimes eliminate the risk of children being born with disabilities. For children who are born with disabilities, the sooner professionals and parents intervene with educational programs, the better.

The IDEA guarantees a free, appropriate public education to all children. When it was originally passed, this law did not specifically require that preschool-aged children be served. Amendments to the legislation either mandated educational services or provided monetary incentives to provide those services. Involving the family in the assessment and treatment of infant and toddlers identified has become a crucial component. An Individualized Family Service Plan (IFSP) must be developed for children from birth through age 2 receiving early intervention services. Part of this chapter involves a look at the advocacy efforts and legislation that affect young children with disabilities today.

There is universal agreement that early identification of actual or potential disabilities is desirable. There is not, however, a universal screening system in use with infants and young children. You should note the interdisciplinary approach to early-childhood screening as well as educational programming. Although medical professionals probably play the most important role in screening for and detecting abnormalities in newborns, parents, teachers, and others are also instrumental in identifying children with disabilities or those who may be at risk of developing specific types of disabilities.

A key point in early intervention is the shift away from assessment instruments and procedures that are based entirely on developmental milestones (the demonstration of certain types of skills at certain ages). Curriculum-based assessment, which links testing, teaching, and new skill acquisition by the child, is becoming more common with young children. In other words, children are being assessed in terms of what they need to be able to do rather than how well their behavior corresponds to age-equivalent norms. As with most of the other areas of exceptionality, teaching skills that will promote independence is critical even for the youngest children.

Ideally, at least part of early childhood special education programming is conducted in the child's home. This is particularly important for very young children. At first glance, special education programming in the home may seem to violate the requirement that services be provided in the least restrictive environment. The home, however, is the natural environment for most toddlers and preschoolers.

Remember, restrictiveness is not defined solely on the basis of the physical site. For many children, the home provides an environment that is nonrestrictive and normalized given the child's age. Three basic program models are described in this chapter. Both home-based and center-based programs have certain advantages and disadvantages. As a result, many programs combine the best features of the two approaches. The use of play for assessment and working on goals has become an integral part of early intervention services.

The curriculum in any special education program should be guided by assessment results. Developmentally based assessment should be used to guide developmentally based curriculum, which, as is discussed in one of the Focus Questions, may not meet the needs of children with severe disabilities. A functional curriculum, consisting of the skills the child needs to acquire, is often the more appropriate choice for young children with disabilities.

Special education is known for its team approach to program planning. Nowhere is this more true or more important than in early childhood special education. A wide variety of professionals are involved with the child and the child's family. The parents not only are encouraged to take an active and vital role in their child's education, they are often the recipients of services themselves. A child's progress might be quite difficult without parental assistance and insight. Both the support provided and needed by parents in early intervention programs are very important, and teachers must be sensitive to individual parents' limits of involvement.

CHAPTER FIVE AT A GLANCE

MAIN TOPICS	KEY POINTS	KEY TERMS	MARGIN NOTES

The Importance of Early Intervention	• Research has documented that early intervention can provide both intermediate and long-term benefits for young children with disabilities and those at risk for developmental delays. Benefits of early intervention include:
	  • Gains in physical development, cognitive development, language and speech development, social competence, and self-help skills
	  • Prevention of secondary disabilities conditions
	  • Reduction of family stress
	  • Reduced need for special education services or placement during the school year
	  • Savings to society of the costs of additional educational and social services that would be needed later in life if early intervention was not provided
	  • Reduced likelihood of social dependence in adulthood
	• The effectiveness of early intervention is increased when it begins early in the child's life, is intensive, and conducted for a long time.
		• early intervention
		• psychosocial disadvantage
			• Early intervention sometimes refers to services provided to infants and toddlers, from birth through age 2, and their families. In this book, the terms **early childhood special education** and **early intervention** are used interchangeably to describe special education services provided to children from birth to age 5.
			• For 15 years the Milwaukee Project provided education and family support services to children born of low-IQ mothers. A book by Garber (1988), the coordinator of the project's research team, describes significant improvements in intelligence, language performance, and academic achievement for the children who received services, compared with a control group of disadvantaged children from mothers of average intelligence.
			• **Psychosocial disadvantage**, a combination of social and environmental deprivation early in a child's life, is generally believed to be the cause of most cases of mild mental retardation.
			• Weisburg (1994) describes a successful early intervention prevention program in which preschoolers from low-income backgrounds received two years of intensive reading instruction based on the Direct Instruction model and materials before they entered kindergarten.

	Key Terms	
Teaching & Learning in School: Selecting Toys for Young Children with Disabilities		• Toys for young children with disabilities should be selected based on their multisensory appeal, method of activation, adjustability, opportunities for success; allowance of self-expression, potential for interaction, safety and durability, where the toy will be used, current popularity, and the child's individual characteristics. • White, Bush, and Casto (1986) conducted a "review of reviews" and found that 94% of a sample of 52 previous reviews of the literature concluded that early intervention resulted in substantial immediate benefits for children with disabilities, those at risk, and those living in impoverished environments.
IDEA and Early Childhood Special Education **Profiles & Perspectives: Educating Young Children Prenatally Exposed to Illegal Drugs**	• developmental delay • establish conditions • Down syndrome • fragile-X syndrome • fetal alcohol syndrome (FAS) • documented risk • biologically at risk • environmentally at risk • sudden infant death syndrome • Individualized Family Service Plan (IFSP)	• IDEA requires states to provide special education services (via IEPs) to all preschool children with disabilities, ages 3 through 5. States may also use IDEA funds to serve infants and toddlers (via IFSPs) birth to age 3 who are experiencing developmental delays or are at risk for acquiring a disability in the future. • Children whose prenatal histories include their mothers' use of drugs are not a homogeneous group, but one that represents a very wide range of abilities. Although prenatal substance exposure may be a factor in explaining the wide-ranging types of problems occurring with greater frequency in our schools, many risk factors associated with living in poverty and less-than-adequate caregiving may also be responsible. No evidence currently exists to suggest that these children exhibit a unique set of problems requiring a special curriculum or set of educational or caregiving procedures. • Smoking during pregnancy and inadequate prenatal care increase the risk of **sudden infant death syndrome (SIDS)**, the leading cause of death in the United States for infants from 1 month to 1 year old. Sleep position is also a risk factor. The incidence of SIDS has dropped sharply in countries that advocate back or side sleeping. The U.S. Department of Health has begun a campaign to encourage parents to put babies to sleep on their back or side. The Back to Sleep Program to increase SIDS prevention and awareness has a toll-free hotline: (800) 505-CRIB. • This provision of IDEA allows, but does not require, states to serve at-risk students from ages 3 through 9 (Turnbull & Cilley, 1999).

	• Although most newborns are evaluated in terms of gestational weight and age and are screened for certain specific disorders, the Apgar scale is at present the only screening test universally used with infants. Another widely practiced screening procedure is the analysis of newborn blood and urine samples to detect metabolic disorders, such as PKU, that produce mental retardation. Many hospitals also routinely analyze newborn blood and urine samples to detect the presence of illegal drugs and other toxins. • Screening tests have also been developed for the early detection of behavioral disorders and autism. Systematic Screening for Behavior Disorders (SSBD) has been adapted for use with preschoolers (Walker, Severson, & Feil, 1994). Two widely used screening instruments for autism are the Autism Behavior Checklist (ABC) (Krug, Arick, & Almond, 1980) and the Childhood Autism Rating Scale (CARS) (Schopler, Reichler, & Renner, 1988). • Parental involvement in screening has been found to reduce the number of misclassifications (Henderson & Meisels, 1994).

Screening, Identification, and Assessment	• Four major types of assessment purposes/tools are used in early childhood special education:
	
	    • Screening involves quick, easy-to-administer tests to identify children who may have a disability and who should receive further testing.
	
	    • Diagnosis requires in depth, comprehensive assessment of all major areas of development to determine a child's eligibility for early intervention or special education services.
	
	    • Program Planning uses curriculum-based, criterion-referenced assessments to determine child's current skill level, identify IFSP/IEP objectives, and plan intervention activities.
	
	    • Evaluation uses curriculum-based, criterion-referenced measures to determine progress on IFSP/IEP objectives and evaluate program's effects.
	
	 • Many early intervention programs are moving away from assessments based entirely on developmental milestones and are incorporating curriculum-based assessment, in which each item relates directly to a skill included in the program's curriculum, which thereby provides a direct link among testing, teaching, and program evaluation.

Curriculum Goals in Early Childhood Special Education		
• Early intervention and education programs for children with special needs should be designed and evaluated according to these outcomes or goals: • Support families in achieving goals. • Promote child engagement, independence, and mastery. • Promote development in all important domains. • Build and support social competence. • Facilitate the generalized use of skills. • Prepare and assist children for normalized life experiences with their families, in school, and in their communities. • Help children and their families make smooth transitions. • Prevent or minimize the development of future problems or disabilities. • Developmentally appropriate practices (DAP) provide a foundation or context within which to provide early intervention for children with special needs, but by themselves the DAP guidelines are inadequate to ensure the individualized intervention such children need. • IEP/IFSP objectives for infants and young children can be evaluated according to their functionality, generality, instructional context, measurability, and relation between short and long-range goals.	• developmentally appropriate practice (DAP)	• Preventative efforts are most effective when intervention services are begun early, conducted systematically and intensively, and provided over a significant period of time (McEachin, Smith, & Lovaas, 1993; Ramey & Ramey, 1992).

Topic	
	• Creating sociodramatic play scripts that require children to interact with one another can be effective in promoting communication skills (Goldstein, 1993). • Even the time between activities can be used for learning and practicing important skills. *Transition-based teaching*, presenting a single instructional trial as a child begins to leave one activity to go to another, has been found effective (Werts et al., 1996; Wolery, Anthony, & Heckathorn, 1998).	• IDEA requires that early intervention services be provided in natural environments to the greatest extent possible. Natural environments are the same home, school, and community settings that typically developing children inhabit (Noonan & McCormick, 1993). • Another model center-based program is the Alice H. Hayden Preschool at the University of Washington.
Teaching & Learning in School: Idea Bunny Helps Preschoolers Be More Independent	• Idea Bunny is an auditory prompting system that has a script of instructions based on a task analysis of each activity. Results from studies have shown that students were able to learn to use the auditory prompt device to complete tasks.
Intervention Strategies in Early Childhood Special Education	• Promoting language development—helping children learn to talk—is a primary curriculum goal for preschoolers with disabilities. The incidental teaching model and the mand-model procedure are two methods for encouraging and developing language use throughout the school day. • Many young children with special needs require instruction to develop social competence.
Service Delivery Alternatives for Early Intervention	• In home-based programs, a child's parents act as the primary teachers, with regular training and guidance from a teacher or specially trained paraprofessional who visits the home. • In center-based programs, a child comes to the center for direct instruction, although the parents are usually involved. Center programs allow a team of specialists to work with the child and enable the child to meet and interact with other children. • Many programs offer the advantages of both models by combining home visits with center-based programming.

	• The Division for Early Childhood recommends specific training and certification requirements for early childhood special educators (DEC, 1993).
Teaching & Learning in School: Including Preschool Children with Autism: Five Strategies That Work	• Teachers should view students holistically and view the outcomes of inclusion and effective instruction broadly when including preschool children with autism. There are five strategies that are central to providing educational services for young children with disabilities in inclusive settings.
Who Can Help?	• A wide range of professionals should be involved in a team that works with young children with disabilities, including obstetricians, pediatricians, nurses, psychologists, social workers, and teachers. • Parents are the most important people in an early intervention program. They can act as advocates, participate in educational planning, observe their children's behavior, help set realistic goals, work in the classroom, and teach their children at home.

CHAPTER FIVE
EARLY CHILDHOOD SPECIAL EDUCATION

Guided Review

I. The Importance of Early Intervention
    A. Early intervention can be defined as a loosely structured confederation of publicly and privately funded home-based and classroom-based efforts that provide:

        1. _____

        2. _____

    B. What are two examples of first-generation research?

        1. _____

        2. _____

    C. What are two examples of second-generation research?

        1. _____

        2. _____

    D. Summarizing the Research Base
        1. What outcomes for early intervention have been identified by IDEA?

            a) _____

            b) _____

            c) _____

            d) _____

            e) _____

II. IDEA and Early Childhood Special Education
    A. What is PL 99-457?

        1. _____

            _____

B. Early Intervention for Infants and Toddlers
    1. The IDEA law covers any child under age 3 who meets the following guidelines:

        a) _____

        b) _____

        c) _____

C. What is an Individualized Family Service Plan?

    1. _____

        _____

D. Special Education for Preschoolers
    1. The regulations governing programs for preschoolers are similar to those for school age children with the following exceptions:

        a) _____

        b) _____

        c) _____

        d) _____

        e) _____

III. Screening, Identification, and Assessment
    A. What are four different purposes for conducting assessment and evaluation?

        1. _____

        2. _____

        3. _____

        4. _____

    B. What are examples of screening tools?

        1. _____

        2. _____

    C. What are two widely used tests for diagnosing developmental delays?

        1. _____

        2. _____

D. Program Planning and Evaluation Tools
  1. Curriculum-based assessment tools enable early childhood teams to:

     a) _____

     b) _____

     c) _____

     d) _____

IV. Curriculum Goals in Early Childhood Special Education
  A. Early childhood special education programs should be designed and evaluated with respect to the following outcomes:

     1. _____

     2. _____

     3. _____

     4. _____

     5. _____

     6. _____

     7. _____

     8. _____

  B. Developmentally Appropriate Practice
     1. What guidelines are recommended for DAP programs?

        a) _____

        b) _____

        c) _____

        d) _____

        e) _____

        f) _____

     2. What are four reasons a curriculum based entirely on DAP may not be sufficient for young children with disabilities?

        a) _____

        b) _____

c) _____

d) _____

C. Selecting IFSP/IEP Objectives
   1. What five criteria should guide the development of objectives?

      a) _____

      b) _____

      c) _____

      d) _____

      e) _____

V. Intervention Strategies in Early Childhood Special Education

   A. Developing Language in Preschoolers with Disabilities
      1. What three things do good teachers do to ensure effective intervention for language-delayed children?

         a) _____

         b) _____

         c) _____

      2. What approaches can teachers use to systematically encourage and develop language throughout the school day?

         a) _____

         b) _____

         c) _____

   B. Promoting the Social Competence of Preschoolers with Disabilities
      1. Peer intervention agents can be taught to make initiations to children with disabilities in the form of:

         a) _____

         b) _____

         c) _____

         d) _____

C. Developing a Preschool Activity Schedule
    1. What are some suggestions for setting up a preschool classroom?

       a) _____

       b) _____

       c) _____

       d) _____

       e) _____

       f) _____

       g) _____

       h) _____

VI. Service Delivery Alternatives for Early Intervention
    A. Hospital-based Programs
    B. Home-based Programs
       1. What are the advantages of home-based programs?

       a) _____

       b) _____

       c) _____

       d) _____

       e) _____

       2. What are the disadvantages of home-based programs?

       a) _____

       b) _____

       c) _____

       d) _____

    C. Center-based programs
       1. What are the advantages of center-based programs?

       a) _____

       b) _____

       c) _____

D. Combined home-center programs
    1. What are the advantages of combined home-center programs?

        a) _____

        b) _____

VII. Who Can Help?
  A. What professionals are involved with the intervention of preschoolers with disabilities?

    1. _____

    2. _____

    3. _____

    4. _____

    5. _____

    6.

  B. Families: Most Important of All
    1. What are the important roles and responsibilities of parents?

        a) _____

        b) _____

        c) _____

        d) _____

        e) _____

        f) _____

CHAPTER FIVE
EARLY CHILDHOOD SPECIAL EDUCATION

Objectives

1. Discuss the various benefits of early intervention.

2. Explain the IDEA mandates for providing services to young children.

3. Describe how an IFSP differs from an IEP.

4. Describe the four major types of assessment used in early childhood special education.

5. Explain the goals of early intervention programs.

6. Explain what is meant by *developmentally appropriate practice*.

7. Explain how IEP/IFSP objectives for infants and young children should be evaluated.

8. Discuss the various types of intervention strategies used in early childhood special education.

9. Identify the types of service delivery programs for young children, and tell the advantages and disadvantages of each.

10. Describe the various types of professionals who are involved in the education of young children with disabilities.

11. Discuss how parents can make the greatest contributions in an early intervention program.

Self-check Quiz

1. PL 99-457 included:
    a. a mandatory preschool component for children ages 3 to 5 and a voluntary incentive grant program for early intervention for infants and toddlers.
    b. a mandatory preschool component for children ages 3 to 5 and mandatory early intervention for infants and toddlers.
    c. a voluntary incentive grant program for children from infancy to age 5.
    d. none of the above

2. Which of the following methodological problems make it difficult to conduct early intervention research in a scientifically sound manner?
    a. selecting meaningful and reliable outcome measures
    b. little variation across early intervention programs
    c. ethical concerns
    d. both a & c

3. _____ provides children with natural, repeated opportunities for critical learning.
   a. Day care
   b. Speech therapy
   c. Play
   d. Early intervention

4. What has been called "the most important legislation ever enacted for developmentally variable children"?
   a. PL 99-457
   b. PL 94-142
   c. American with Disabilities Act (ADA)
   d. PL 105-17

5. What are the three categories of eligibility stated in the Individuals with Disabilities Education Act (IDEA) under which states can provide early intervention services to infants and toddlers?
   a. established conditions, cognitive development, and documented risk
   b. developmental delay, established conditions, and documented risk
   c. developmental delay, documented risk, and cognitive development
   d. cognitive development, developmental delay, established conditions

6. Curriculum-based, criterion-referenced measures to determine progress on IFSP/IEP objectives is called:
   a. screening.
   b. diagnosis.
   c. program planning.
   d. evaluation.

7. The Apgar scale:
   a. measures the degree of prenatal oxygen deprivation.
   b. measures the degree of prematurity.
   c. is only administered to low-birth-weight babies.
   d. all of the above

8. What is the most widely used screening tool for developmental delays?
   a. Denver II
   b. Battelle Developmental Inventory
   c. Bayley Scales of Infant Development II
   d. Assessment, Evaluation, and Programming System

9. The Idea Bunny helps preschoolers develop:
   a. social skills.
   b. generalization.
   c. language development.
   d. independent performance skills.

10. What is the basic measure of success for language intervention?
    a. extensive vocabulary used by the child
    b. articulation in speech
    c. how much the child talks
    d. child speaks when spoken to

11. A preschooler with delayed language stands in front of the teacher with a broken toy and starts to cry. The teacher asks, "What happened to the toy?" What method is the teacher using?
    a. Milieu instructional approach
    b. Incidental teaching
    c. Functionality method
    d. Mand model

12. Cindy is using the computer. The teacher asks, "Cindy, what program are you working with?" What method is the teacher using to promote language development?
    a. Milieu instructional approach
    b. Incidental teaching
    c. Functionality method
    d. Mand model

13. The IFSP must be:
    a. evaluated once a year.
    b. reviewed with the family at 6-month intervals.
    c. reviewed with the family at 3-month intervals.
    d. both a & b

14. Developmentally Appropriate Practice (DAP) recommends all of the following guidelines for early childhood education programs EXCEPT:
    a. The teacher should arrange the environment to facilitate active exploration.
    b. The children's interests and progress should be identified by using assessment tools.
    c. The complexity and challenges of activities should increase as the children understand the skills involved.
    d. Learning activities should be real, concrete, and relevant to the child.

15. Developmentally Appropriate Practice (DAP):
    a. targets specific goals and objectives to meet the unique developmental needs of individual children.
    b. uses comprehensive and repeated assessments to develop objectives.
    c. may not be sufficient for children with disabilities.
    d. all of the above

CHAPTER SIX
MENTAL RETARDATION

Focus Questions

• **What is most important in determining a person's level of adaptive functioning: intellectual capability or a supportive environment?**

As you contemplate this question, think about the quality of life of individuals called mentally retarded. Which factor is more likely to determine whether or not an individual has access to and can function in various school, work, and residential settings? Is it how bright he or she is, or how much support he or she receives? Or is it both? For example, Faye, a young adult with mental retardation, is part of a mobile crew cleaning offices in a large downtown office complex. As Faye's teacher and supervisor, you know her to be a capable worker. She cleans, sweeps, dusts, and performs all her other job-related tasks fluently. The supervisor of her mobile work crew, however, does not believe in providing varied levels of support for his employees, so Faye is not being successful at her job. As Faye's teacher what should you do? Should you try to improve her abilities or find a more supportive environment for employment?

• **What should a curriculum for students with mental retardation emphasize?**

Not all students labeled mentally retarded have the same abilities or interests. Each student's program should be designed to fit his or her unique needs. Today, there are many different educational and residential placement options available. In general, however, functional skills that will lead to the child's independence in the community and workplace should be the focus of most educational programs for individuals with mental retardation.

• **What are the characteristics of effective instruction?**

There are six features to effective teaching which are based on the scientific method: (a) precise definition and task analysis of the new skill or behavior to be learned, (b) direct and frequent measurement of the student's performance of the skill, (c) frequent opportunities for active student response during instruction, (d) immediate and systematic feedback for student performance, (e) procedures for achieving the transfer of stimulus control from instructional cues or prompts to naturally occurring stimuli, and (f) strategies for promoting the generalization and maintenance of newly learned skills to different, nontraining situations and environments.

• **Is inclusion a good thing for every student with mental retardation?**

Not necessarily. Simply placing a child with disabilities into a regular classroom does not guarantee that student will be accepted socially or receive the most appropriate and needed instructional programming. Factors which may determine the success of an inclusive placement in a regular classroom include: the child's level of functioning, the teacher's ability to individualize instruction and make appropriate accommodations, the degree of support and collaboration with other professionals, the extent of parent involvement, and the level of peer maturity.

- **How can environmental supports, the principle of normalization, and self-determination interact to influence successful functioning in the community?**

  The principle of normalization refers to the use of progressively more normal settings and procedures to establish and/or maintain personal behaviors which are as culturally normal as possible. This principle suggests that the environmental supports used to educate individuals with mental retardation should be as typical as possible to help facilitate integration or inclusion efforts. A large part of successful independent living is being able to meet the performance expectations in our communities.

Chapter Overview

Words such as *helpless, unteachable, dependent,* and *childlike* are often associated with people with mental retardation. Less often are people with mental retardation described with positive characteristics, such as *hardworking, capable, independent,* and *productive.* Yet, many children and adults with mental retardation are just that: hard-working, capable, independent, and productive members of classrooms and communities. Some individuals with mental retardation, certainly, are not as capable as others, but this same statement can be made about any group of people.

The chapter begins by discussing the ever-changing definition of mental retardation. Several definitions of mental retardation have been proposed, debated, revised and counterproposed over the years. Mental retardation is a complex concept that is difficult to define. It involves significant deficits in both intellectual functioning and adaptive behavior—both of which are difficult to measure. Even the slightest rewording in the definition can influence who is considered mentally retarded and consequently, who is eligible for special education services. The most recent definition of mental retardation moves away from deficits within the individual toward levels of support needed in the environment for the individual to function effectively.

There are more than 250 known causes of mental retardation, but, for the majority of individuals, the exact cause is unknown. All of the known causes of retardation are biological or medical. The chapter briefly reviews recent scientific advances that are helping to decrease the incidence of clinical retardation including genetic counseling, amniocentesis, and virus vaccines. In addition, provided in the chapter are descriptions of effective instructional methodologies for these students including the use of a task analysis to target skills to be taught, direct and frequent measurement of learner's performance, instructional strategies which provide increased active student responding, effective use of systematic feedback, strategies for transferring stimulus control, and techniques for promoting generalization and maintenance of skills.

Recent developments in instructional technology provide evidence that individuals with mental retardation can learn skills previously thought beyond their capability. Some children with mental retardation attend special public schools or live in institutional settings. More and more, however, are being educated in their neighborhood schools and are living in neighborhood settings where they make valuable contributions to their communities.

CHAPTER SIX AT A GLANCE

MAIN TOPICS	KEY POINTS	KEY TERMS	MARGIN NOTES
Defining Mental Retardation	• The definition incorporated into IDEA states that mental retardation involves both significantly subaverage general intellectual functioning and deficits in adaptive behavior manifested between birth and age 18. Intellectual functioning is usually measured with a standardized intelligence test and adaptive behavior with an observation checklist or scale. • The most recent AAMR definition of mental retardation, the "1992 System," represents a shift away from conceptualizations of mental retardation as an inherent trait or permanent state of being to a description of the individual's present functioning and the environmental supports needed to improve it. • There are four degrees of mental retardation as classified by IQ score: mild, moderate, severe, and profound. • Children with mild mental retardation may experience substantial performance deficits only in school. Their social and communication skills may be normal or nearly so. They are likely to become independent or semi-independent adults. • Most children with moderate mental retardation show significant developmental delays during their preschool years, are educated in self-contained classrooms, and most live and work in the community as adults if individualized programs of support are available.	• mental retardation • normal curve • standard deviation • dynamic assessment • criterion-referenced test • adaptive behavior • etiology • educable mentally retarded (EMR) • trainable mentally retarded (TMR) • estimated learning potential (ELP)	• The term **mental retardation** is, above all, a label used to identify an observed performance deficit—failure to demonstrate age-appropriate intellectual and social behavior. Mental retardation describes performance; it is not a "thing" that a person is born with or possesses. • AAMR is an interdisciplinary organization of professionals as well as students, parents, and others concerned with the study, treatment, and prevention of mental retardation. Its more than 9,500 members are from 55 countries. • An earlier definition published by AAMR (Heber, 1961) required an IQ score of only one standard deviation below the mean for the diagnosis of mental retardation. • A standardized test consists of the same questions and tasks always presented in a certain, specified way, with the same scoring procedures used each time the test is administered. An IQ test has also been normed—that is, administered to a large sample of people selected at random from the population for whom the test is intended. Test scores of the people in the random sample are then used as norms, or averages of how people generally perform on the test. • The AAMR manual emphasizes that the IQ cutoff of 70 is intended only as a guideline and should not be interpreted as a hard-and-fast requirement. A higher IQ score of 75 or more may be associated with mental retardation if, according to a clinician's judgment, the child exhibits deficits in adaptive behavior thought to be caused by impaired intellectual functioning.

- A possible negative outcome of being labeled as mentally retarded is that peers may be more likely to avoid or ridicule the child.

- Traditional methods of standardized assessment do not allow the examiner to give prompts or cues or to interact in any way that might "teach" the child how to respond correctly during the test itself. Some psychologists and educators believe that such strict testing methods do not reveal the child's true learning potential. They recommend an alternative approach to assessment called *dynamic assessment* in which the examiner uses various forms of guided learning activities to determine the child's potential for change.

- A *criterion-referenced test* for basic math skills, for example, might include 10 single-digit addition problems. Rather than judging the child's ability to compute single-digit math problems by comparing his performance with other children's or inferring it from his work on other types of math problems, the child's performance on the skill in question is compared with a standard criterion. For example, if the criterion is 9 and the child gets 9 or 10 correct, instruction will not be necessary on that skill; if he gets fewer than 9 correct, a teaching program for single-digit addition problems would be implemented.

- The ABS-S is long: 104 items with multiple questions per item. A shorter (75-item) adaptation of the scale, called the Classroom Adaptive Behavior Checklist, has been developed by Hunsucker, Nelson, and Clark (1986). Another form, the ABS-RC, assesses adaptive behavior in residential and community settings (Nihira et al., 1993).

Profiles & Perspectives: Positive Expectations and 10,000 Hours

- Most persons with severe and profound mental retardation are identified in infancy. Some adults with severe and profound mental retardation can be semi-independent; others need 24-hour support throughout their lives.

- Classification in the AAMR's "1992 System" is based on four levels and intensities of supports needed to improve functioning in the environments in which the individual lives: intermittent, limited, extensive, and pervasive.

- Parents of a child with Down syndrome spent 10,000 hours working with their son before he was 5. They were challenged to find different approaches to effectively teach their son. They attribute his success to positive expectations.

	• An examination of the guidelines issued by state departments of education found that only 56% of states used the term *mental retardation*; the remaining states classified students with terms such as *developmental disabilities, developmental handicaps,* or *mental disabilities* (Utley, Lowitzer, & Baumeister, 1987). • Carroll, Burnworth, Chambers, Cousino, Mahaney, and Trent (1991) describe how students with disabilities can learn needed functional academic and vocational skills by operating a "classroom company." • Mental retardation is seldom a time-limited condition. Although many individuals with mental retardation make tremendous advancements in adaptive skills (some to the point of functioning independently and no longer being considered under any disability category), most are affected throughout their life span (Mulick & Antonak, 1994).	• Prevalence rates vary greatly from state to state. For example, the prevalence of mental retardation as a percentage of total school enrollment ranged from a low of 0.28% (New Jersey) to a high of 2.52% (Alabama). Such large differences in prevalence are no doubt a function of the widely differing criteria for identifying students with mental retardation (Frankenberger & Fronzaglio, 1991). Prevalence figures also vary considerably among districts within a given state (McDermott, 1994).
Prevalence	• Theoretically, 2.3% of the population would score two standard deviations below the norm on IQ tests, but this does not account for adaptive behavior, the other criterion for diagnosis of mental retardation. Many experts now cite an incidence figure of approximately 1% of the total population. • During the 1994-1995 school year, approximately 1% of the total school enrollment received special education services under the disability category of mental retardation.

Topic	Content	Key Terms	
Causes of Mental Retardation	• All of the more than 250 known causes of mental retardation are biological. • Etiology is unknown for most individuals with mild mental retardation. Increasing evidence, however, suggests that psychosocial disadvantages in early childhood is a major cause of mild mental retardation.	• prenatal • perinatal • postnatal • clinical mental retardation • developmental retardation • longitudinal study	• The term *syndrome* refers to a number of symptoms that occur together and that provide the defining characteristics of a given disease or condition. Down syndrome and fragile-X syndrome are the most common causes of inherited mental retardation. • The term *developmental retardation* is also used as a synonym for *psychosocial disadvantage* to refer to mental retardation thought to be caused primarily by environmental influences such as minimal opportunities to develop early language, child abuse and neglect, and/or chronic social or sensory deprivation. • A **longitudinal study** follows the development of the same subjects over a period of years.
Educational Approaches	• Curriculum should focus on functional skills that will help the student be successful in self-care, vocational, domestic, community, and leisure domains. • Applied behavior analysis is widely used in teaching students with mental retardation. Major components include task analysis, direct and frequent measurement, repeated opportunities to respond, systematic feedback, transfer of stimulus control from teacher-provided cues and prompts to natural stimuli, and programming for generalization and maintenance.	• applied behavior analysis • task analysis • precision teaching • active student response (ASR) • choral responding • response cards • guided notes • time trials • acquisition stage of learning • practice stage of learning • fluency • positive reinforcement	• A task-analytic procedure based on 17 fundamental motions known as *therbligs* can also be used by special educators (Browder, Lim, Lin, & Belfiore, 1993). • **Precision teaching** is a method of direct and frequent assessment of student performance with specific decision rules indicating when instruction should be modified. • Several studies have found that *instructive feedback* can increase the efficiency of instruction for students with mental retardation and other disabilities (Werts, Wolery, Gast, & Holcombe, 1996). When giving feedback to students on their responses to targeted items, the teacher intentionally and methodically presents extra information.
Teaching & Learning in School: How Many Can You Do in One Minute?	• Accuracy measures alone do not provide a complete picture of learning. Students with disabilities need practice to build fluency through activities like time trials.		

	Recent studies have found that individuals with mental retardation can use self-operated prompting systems to help learn and perform a variety of academic, domestic, and vocational tasks (e.g., Barfels, Heward, & Al-Attrash, 1999; Briggs et al., 1990; Grossi, 1998; Mechling & Gast, 1997). • Constant time delay may sound like a difficult procedure, but it's not. One study found that second- and fourth-grade students could successfully use constant time delay to teach sight words to three peers with mental retardation and other disabilities (Wolery, Werts, Snyder, & Caldwell, 1994). • Generalization and maintenance of skills in the regular classroom can be enhanced by training students with disabilities to recruit teacher praise and attention for their good behavior (Alber & Heward, 1997).	• instructive feedback • learning trial • stimulus control • constant time delay • generalization • maintenance
Teaching & Learning in School: What to Do When Students Make Mistakes	• It is important that feedback be provided before the student is required to use the skill/knowledge again. Error correction will be more effective if done before going to the next item, related to the target skill, short and concise, and provided in the form of hints or probes.	
Educational Placement Alternatives	• Most children with mental retardation are educated in their neighborhood schools—either in special classes or in regular classes—where they receive special help or attend a resource room for part of the day. • Many children with mental retardation are educated in regular classrooms, with extra help provided as needed. They can generally master standard academic skills up to about a sixth-grade level. • Students with moderate mental retardation are usually taught communication, self-help and daily living skills, and vocational skills, along with limited academics mainly in self-contained classrooms.	

		• Wolf Wolfensberger (1983), the best-known champion of the normalization principle, has proposed the term *social role valorization* to replace *normalization*. He writes, "The most explicit and highest goal of normalization must be the creation, support, and defense of valued social roles for people who are at risk of social devaluation" (p. 234).
		• advocate • genetic counseling • amniocentesis • chorion villus sampling • normalization
Teaching & Learning in School: Some Things We've Learned About Inclusion	• Despite their severe disabilities, people with severe and profound mental retardation can learn. Curricula stress functional communication and self-help skills. • Most benefits of inclusion depend on how schools plan for, implement, and support change and then sustain outcomes.	
Current Issues and Future Trends	• Recent laws have extended and affirmed the rights of persons with mental retardation. Advocates can help protect the rights of individuals with mental retardation. • Recent scientific advances—including genetic counseling, amniocentesis, CVS, virus vaccines, and early screening tests—are helping reduce the incidence of clinical or biologically caused retardation. • Although early identification and intensive educational services to high-risk infants show promise, there is still no widely used technique to decrease the incidence of mental retardation caused by psychosocial disadvantage. • The current goal is to make the lives of people with mental retardation—at home, in school, and at work—as normal as possible. Institutions are necessarily inappropriate. Thus, we must develop normalized and effective training and transition programs and community services for individuals with mental retardation and work to change public attitude.	

CHAPTER SIX
MENTAL RETARDATION

Guided Review _____

I. Defining Mental Retardation
A. What are the three components of AAMR's IQ-Based Definition?

1. _____

2. _____

3. _____

B. Measuring Intellectual Functioning
1. What is the normal curve?

a) _____

2. What is the standard deviation?

a) _____

3. What are the two most widely used IQ tests?

a) _____

b) _____

C. Support of the Shift to IQ 70
1. Why is there a shift to a more conservative definition of MR?

a) _____

b) _____

c) _____

d) _____

2. What are the advantages and disadvantages of IQ tests?

a) _____

b) _____

c) _____

d) _____

e) _____

f) _____

g) _____

D. Measuring Adaptive Behavior
1. What is the definition of adaptive behavior?

a) _____

_____

2. What instruments are used for assessing adaptive behavior?

a) _____

b) _____

c) _____

E. Classifying MR Based on Intellectual Ability
1. How does the most widely used method classify students with MR?

a) _____

b) _____

c) _____

d) _____

2. What are the important outcomes of special education for children with Mild Mental Retardation?

a) _____

b) _____

c) _____

3. What are the characteristics of people with Moderate Mental Retardation?

a) _____

b) _____

4. What are the characteristics of people with Severe and Profound Mental Retardation?

a) _____

b) _____

c) _____

F. What are the Alternative Definitions of Mental Retardation that Emphasize Individualized Need for Supports?

1. _____

2. _____

3. _____

4. _____

G. AAMR's Definition Based on Needed Supports: The 1992 System
   1. What four assumptions are essential to the application of this definition?

   a) _____

   b) _____

   c) _____

   d) _____

H. Classification Based on Intensity of Needed Supports
   1. What are the four intensities of supports?

   a) _____

   b) _____

   c) _____

   d) _____

   2. What are the four dimensions of types and intensity of needed supports?

   a) _____

   b) _____

   c) _____

   d) _____

I. Criticisms of the AAMR's New Definition of Mental Retardation
   1. What are the concerns of the new definition?

   a) _____

b) _____

c) _____

d) _____

e) _____

II. Prevalence
   A. Why is it difficult to estimate the number of people with mental retardation?

      1. _____

   B. A recent national study estimated the prevalence rate of mental retardation at _____ percent of the U.S. population.

   C. How many students ages 6 through 21 received special education under the disability category of mental retardation during the 1996-1997 school year?

      1. _____

III. Causes of Mental Retardation
   A. How are the causes of MR classified?

      1. _____

      2. _____

      3. _____

   B. What are organic causes?

      1. _____

   C. Environmental Causes
      1. What are the key contributors to environmental MR?

         a) _____

         b) _____

         c) _____

         d) _____

IV. Educational Approaches
   A. Curriculum Goals
      1. Functional Academics
         a) What questions should be asked to determine appropriate functional goals?

            1) _____

               _____

2) _____

3) _____

4) _____

5) _____

6) _____

2. Community Living Skills
   a) What are the five domains of community living skills?

   1) _____

   2) _____

   3) _____

   4) _____

   5) _____

B. Instructional Methodology
   1. What are the six features of teaching practices based on Applied Behavior Analysis?

   a) _____

   b) _____

   c) _____

   d) _____

   e) _____

   f) _____

   2. What is task analysis?

   a) _____

   3. What is direct and frequent measurement?

   a) _____

   4. What are some strategies for increasing active student response?

   a) _____

   b) _____

c) _____

d) _____

e) _____

f) _____

g) _____

h) _____

5. Systematic Feedback
   a) What are the critical variables of effective feedback?

   1) _____

   2) _____

   3) _____

   4) _____

   5) _____

   b) What are the elements of a learning trial?

   1) _____

   2) _____

   3) _____

   c) What are the two stages of learning?

   1) _____

   2) _____

6. Transfer of Stimulus Control
   a) What is one method for transferring stimulus control?

   1) _____

7. Generalization and Maintenance
   a) What are strategies for promoting generalization and maintenance?

   1) _____

   2) _____

   3) _____

   4) _____

V. Educational Placement Alternatives
    A. In what settings have students with MR been educated during the 1995-96 school year?

        1. _____% in the regular classroom

        2. _____% in the resource room

        3. _____% in separate classes

VI. What Are the Current Issues and Future Trends for Individuals with MR?

    A. _____

    B. _____

    C. _____

CHAPTER SIX
MENTAL RETARDATION

Objectives

1. Explain the IDEA and AAMR definitions of mental retardation.

2. Explain what is meant by *adaptive behavior*.

3. Describe the four following levels of service intensity: intermittent, limited, extensive, and pervasive.

4. Identify the prevalence of children with mental retardation.

5. Explain the causes of mental retardation.

6. Describe the functional skills necessary for independent functioning.

7. Describe the components of Applied Behavior Analysis.

8. Explain the educational placement alternatives for children with mental retardation.

9. Describe the recent scientific advances that may help reduce the incidence of clinical mental retardation.

10. Discuss how recent laws have influenced the rights of individuals with mental retardation.

Self-check Quiz

1. Significantly subaverage intelligence and poor academic performance must be present to classify students as mentally retarded. What other variable must be present for the classification?
   a. a biological or genetic condition
   b. deficits in adaptive behavior
   c. a discrepancy between achievement and ability
   d. distractibility and hyperactivity in any context

2. An IQ test is an example of a:
   a. criterion-referenced test.
   b. standardized test.
   c. norm-referenced test.
   d. both b & c

3. What is a critical factor for determining the supports which individuals with mental retardation may require for success in school, work, and residential settings?
   a. severity of maladaptive behavior
   b. IQ score
   c. grades in school
   d. nutritional factors

4. Ms. Richards has referred the following four students to the school psychologist for evaluations. Which child is more likely than the others to be identified as having mental retardation?
   a. Erin shows low levels of achievement in all academic areas and prefers to play with much younger children.
   b. Jenny is having trouble in mathematics but is performing at grade level in all other subjects.
   c. Terrence is hyperactive and often daydreams during independent work time.
   d. Jerry is a low achiever in all areas, and he is a leader of a local gang.

5. The causes of most cases of mental retardation are:
   a. unknown.
   b. known to be biological or medical.
   c. presumed to be environmental.
   d. both a & c

6. Which of the following is a true statement?
   a. IQ tests have proven to be the best single predictor of school achievement.
   b. IQ scores cannot change significantly.
   c. Results of an IQ test are useful for determining instructional strategies.
   d. both a & c

7. What is the estimated prevalence rate of mental retardation in the United States?
   a. 2.5%
   b. 1%
   c. 28%
   d. 3%

8. A longitudinal study of 45 infants and their families examined the relationship between socioeconomic status (SES) and parent-child interactions (Hart & Risley, 1995). The results of this study indicate:
   a. a strong correlation between SES status and amount of exposure to language in the home.
   b. children from lower-SES households received more exposure to language at 7 to 36 months of age than did middle- or upper-SES children.
   c. children from middle- and upper-SES families received more verbal interactions than did the lower-SES children.
   d. both a & c

9. What question should be asked when determining whether or not any given skill represents functional curriculum?
   a. "Will he need it when he is 21 years old?"
   b. "Can he learn to do it in a year?"
   c. "Will it teach him survival vocabulary?"
   d. "Can his parents teach it at home?"

10. Which of the following is NOT a feature of behavior analysis?
    a. direct and frequent measurement
    b. frequent opportunities for active student response
    c. diagnosing the specific disability category
    d. immediate and systematic feedback

11. Ms. Goldenberg teaches in a special education resource room. She often uses the same textbooks, materials, rules, and homework assignments used in the regular classroom. She is teaching for:
    a. generalization.
    b. reinforcement.
    c. acquisition.
    d. feedback.

12. Which of the following teachers is using an instructional strategy which increases active student responding?
    a. Mr. Chinn requires his sixth graders to follow his social studies lecture by using guided notes.
    b. Ms. Zilkes calls on individual students to answer science review questions.
    c. Mr. Rourk rewards the whole class with 5 extra minutes of recess if they all pay attention during math instruction.
    d. all of the above

13. Ms. Shea has begun to gradually withdraw the verbal prompt of "Raise your hand" after she asks a question so that the students will eventually raise their hands after she asks a question without the verbal prompt. This is an example of:
    a. generalization training.
    b. maintenance training.
    c. transferring stimulus control.
    d. systematic feedback.

14. Which of the following teachers is using time trials appropriately?
    a. After Mr. Willard's students acquired basic multiplication facts, he conducted one 10-minute trial every other day for three weeks.
    b. After Ms. McKinley's students acquired basic multiplication facts, she conducted three 1-minute trials every day for three weeks.
    c. Ms. Hatch began conducting 1-minute time trials daily beginning the first day she taught basic multiplication facts.
    d. both b & c

15. Which of the following is a volunteer committed to becoming personally involved with the welfare of a person with a disability and knowledgeable about the services available for that person?
    a. an advocate
    b. a lawyer
    c. a lobbyist
    d. a special education teacher

CHAPTER SEVEN
LEARNING DISABILITIES

Focus Questions _____

- **Why has the concept of learning disabilities proven so difficult to define?**

There are many different types of academic and social skills students are expected to learn during their formal education and an infinite range of individual differences among learners in any given classroom. No two children will learn the same skill at exactly the same rate or to the exact same level of accuracy, proficiency, maintenance, or generalization. In one sense, all students could be said to be learning disabled in relation to some level of "standard" performance. The field of learning disabilities has struggled to describe the defining characteristics of this disability since its beginnings as a formal area of special education. There are subtle differences of intent and emphasis by the various individuals and groups who have proposed definitions. Defining what is often a hidden or "school-hours-only" disability remains a challenge to the field of special education. Regardless of the quality of a categorical definition representing the learning difficulties students experience in school, the definition itself will provide the classroom teacher with little useful information about how to teach or what skills need to be taught to a particular student. It is quite important that the majority of educational professionals' efforts are devoted to the development and delivery of effective instruction rather than debates over definitions.

- **Do most students who are identified as learning disabled have a true disability? Or are they just low achievers or victims of poor instruction?**

They are probably both. Learning disabilities are considered by some to be a school-defined phenomenon because the disability is most commonly exhibited through difficulties in acquiring and mastering academic skills. It is important to remember, however, that the process of learning how to read or do mathematics is not fundamentally different from learning how to drive a car, operate a computer, drive a nail, or make a friend. While learning disabilities are often specific to certain kinds of skills, many individuals have difficulty learning across a wide range of settings and skills. It is also important to remember that the student who has experienced difficulties in learning throughout his or her school years will not magically lose this disability upon graduation. The learning disability will change only in the sense that the skills to be learned are different.

- **What are the most important skills for an elementary-age student with learning disabilities to master? A secondary student?**

One of the fundamental goals of any special education program is to help integrate each exceptional child into the mainstream of society as much as possible. Children with learning disabilities need to learn the same kinds of basic skills as other children that will enable them to experience success in academic, vocational, and social situations. In other words, skills that are important for non-learning disabled children are equally important for children with learning disabilities. As students with learning disabilities get older, different teaching settings and/or different instructional priorities may be warranted. Instruction may, for example, need to focus less on basic skills and concentrate more on such skills as learning strategies and self-management techniques. As with any category of disability, instruction must change to meet the changing needs of the student.

- **How do basic academic skills and learning strategies relate to each other?**

A learning strategy can be defined as "an individual's approach to a learning task. A strategy includes how a person thinks and acts when planning, executing, and evaluating performance on a task and its' outcomes." They need to be explicitly taught to students with a learning disability. Improvement in academic skills can result when learning strategies are applied.

- **Should all students with learning disabilities be educated in the regular classroom?**

The regular education classroom with non-disabled same-age peers currently represents the least restrictive environment for most students with learning disabilities. Does this, however, mean that all students with learning disabilities have "mild" disabilities. Many, if not the majority of, educators, parents, and advocacy groups have raised a number of concerns about the movement toward full inclusion and its impact on placement options and a continuum of services for students with learning disabilities. They have argued that for some students, the regular classroom may be quite restrictive. At question is the degree to which an appropriate individualized education can be guaranteed for students with learning disabilities who receive all instruction in the regular classroom. The debate has created a curious irony for the field of special education. On one hand, the field is based on legal and philosophical premises requiring students with disabilities to receive their education in the least restrictive environment. On the other hand, some advocates for students with learning disabilities fear that should full inclusion become a reality for all students with LD, the field of learning disabilities will cease to exist. All discussions about placement options and the relative restrictiveness of a given placement should focus on the needs of the student. The special educators of the future, perhaps those currently studying this text, will be the ones who will determine the direction of the field. Professionals, parents, and advocates must insure that the debate, while important, serves the right constituency—learners with disabilities; and that the ultimate outcome of the debate accomplishes improved educational opportunity, instructional practice, and meaningful outcomes for all students.

Chapter Overview

There is no standard, universally accepted definition of what constitutes a learning disability. However, the fundamental, defining characteristics of students with learning disabilities are: specific and significant achievement deficiency in the presence of adequate overall intelligence. Speculation about causes, different terminology used by different professions (medical, psychological, and educational), and diverse approaches to instruction all complicate the field of learning disabilities. One standard practice does exist, however. Teachers of children with learning disabilities are putting more emphasis on instructional programming and less emphasis on labels and causes.

Assessment is essential to planning an instructional program to teach the skills a child needs to acquire. Students with learning disabilities are the most tested group of students in the schools. Many types of tests are used in the process of identifying and teaching children with learning disabilities. Testing, however, is not teaching. Too often, educators get bogged down with testing and never quite get around to acting on the test results.

Using assessment information to improve instruction is at the heart of "best practice" in educating students with learning disabilities. Approaches such as explicit instruction, content enhancements, and learning strategies have been identified as effective means of teaching students with learning disabilities. Direct Instruction programs consist of carefully scripted, field-tested lessons in which students respond, both chorally and individually, to a fast-paced series of learning tasks presented by the teacher. Careful selection and sequencing of tasks in the lessons helps students systematically acquire important background knowledge so they can explicitly apply it and link it to new knowledge. Content enhancements, such as graphic organizers, visual displays, guided notes, and mnemonic strategies help make curriculum content more accessible to students with learning disabilities. Learning strategies help students guide themselves successfully through specific tasks or general problems.

Children with disabilities must be educated in the least restrictive environment. Nearly all children with learning disabilities are taught in regular school buildings and to a large extent in regular classrooms. Although some children's learning problems are so severe that they require full-time special class instruction, other children, whose learning problems are less severe, require only limited special education services to succeed in full-time mainstream placements. Because most students with learning disabilities spend at least part of each school day in the regular classroom, a great deal of cooperative planning is required of the regular and special education teachers. Collaboration and consultation with general education teachers is an important part of the responsibilities of the teacher of students with learning disabilities.

All children have difficulty learning at one time or another or to one degree or another. An understanding of this field is therefore important for all teachers, because they are likely to meet children with learning disabilities in their own classroom one day.

CHAPTER SEVEN AT A GLANCE

MAIN TOPICS	KEY POINTS	KEY TERMS	MARGIN NOTES
Defining Learning Disabilities	• There is no universally agreed-on definition of learning disabilities. Most states require that three criteria be met: (a) a severe discrepancy between potential or ability and actual achievement, (b) learning problems that cannot be attributed to other disabilities, and (c) need special educational services to succeed in school. • No matter which definition is used, educators should focus on each student's specific skill deficiencies for assessment and instruction.	• dyslexia • minimal brain dysfunction • perceptual impairments • developmental aphasia	• The term *learning disabilities* was coined by Samuel Kirk in an address in 1963 to a group of parents whose children were experiencing serious difficulties in learning to read, were hyperactive, or could not solve math problems. • The NJCLD's requirement that the disorder is "intrinsic to the individual and presumed to be due to central nervous system dysfunction" can be seen as an effort to limit the use of the term *learning disabilities* to the "hard-core" or severely learning disabled. • Mercer, Jordan, Allsopp, and Mercer (1995) surveyed all 50 states and found that the majority uses the IDEA definition of learning disabilities or some variation of it. • Fuchs and Fuchs (1998) describe how curriculum-based measurement can be used to distinguish students with learning disabilities from students whose low achievement is due primarily to ineffective instruction.
Characteristics of Students with Learning Disabilities	• Most students with learning disabilities show one or more of the following characteristics: reading problems, deficits in written language, underachievement in math, social skills deficits, problems with attention and hyperactivity, and behavioral problems. • The fundamental, defining characteristic of students with learning disabilities is specific and significant achievement deficiency in the presence of adequate overall intelligence.	• minimal brain dysfunction • dyslexia • attention-deficit hyperactivity disorder (ADHD) • Diagnostic and Statistical Manual of Mental Disorders (DSM-IV)	• Early in the field's history a task force commissioned to identify the characteristics of children with learning disabilities (the term **minimal brain dysfunction** was used to describe these children at that time) found that 99 separate characteristics were reported in the literature (Clements, 1966). • The term **dyslexia** is also used to refer to reading disabilities. For a discussion and definition of dyslexia as a distinct type of learning disability, see Lyon (1995).

	• Specific recommendations for teaching writing to exceptional students can be found in *For Ideas on How to Help Students Use the Internet to Improve Their Writing Skills*, see Smith, Bone and Higgins (1998). • The winter and spring 1996 issues of *LD Forum* are devoted to teaching math to students with learning disabilities. • Another interpretation is that the concept of learning disabilities is poorly defined and functions as a catch-all category for any student who is experiencing learning problems and who does not meet eligibility requirements for other disability categories. • Howell, Evans and Gardiner (1997) provide educators with guidelines for the safe use of stimulant medications in the classroom with optimal benefits. • Regardless of the interrelationships of these characteristics, teachers and other caregivers responsible for planning educational programs for students with learning disabilities need skills in dealing with social and behavioral difficulties as well as academic deficits.
Teaching & Learning in School: Six Principles for Early Reading Instruction	• There are six key principles of effective beginning reading instruction: (1) begin teaching phonemic awareness directly at an early age (kindergarten); (2) teach each letter-phoneme relationship explicitly; (3) teach frequent, highly regular letter-sound relationships systematically; (4) show children exactly how to sound out words; (5) give children connected, decodable text to practice the letter-phoneme relationships; and (6) use interesting stories to develop language comprehension.

Prevalence	Learning disabilities is the largest category in special education. Students with learning disabilities represent about 5% of the total school enrollment in the United States and half of all students receiving special education.		Males outnumber females by a 3-to-1 ratio across primary, elementary, and secondary age levels (Cone et al., 1985; McLeskey, 1992). During this same period, the percentage of school-age students receiving special education services under the category of mental retardation dropped from approximately 1 in every 4 students in 1976–77 to 1 in 9 students in 1995–96.
Causes of Learning Disabilities	Although the actual cause of a specific learning disability is seldom known, four types of suspected causal factors are brain damage, heredity, biochemical imbalance, and environmental factors such as impoverished child-rearing practices and poor instruction.	minimal brain dysfunction	Although it is possible, or even probable, that biochemistry may affect a student's behavior and learning in the classroom, no reliable scientific evidence exists today revealing the nature or extent of that influence. Rooney (1991), who reviewed and critiqued a number of controversial therapies claiming to cure or remediate the learning and/or behavioral problems experienced by children with disabilities, suggests that we "read the fine print" before accepting a discovery.
Assessment	Norm-referenced tests compare a child's score with the scores of other age-mates who have taken the same test. Criterion-referenced tests, which compare a child's score with a predetermined mastery level, are useful in identifying specific skills the child has learned as well as skills that require instruction. Teachers use informal reading inventories to directly observe and record a child's reading skills.	norm-referenced tests; criterion-referenced tests; informal reading inventory; curriculum-based assessment; Precision teaching; Standard Celeration Chart	In the 1960s and 1970s, tests designed to assess psycholinguistic, perceptual-motor, or visual-perceptual abilities were often used with children with learning disabilities. Such process tests are seldom used today; research has shown that instruction designed to improve the abilities assessed by the tests is ineffective (e.g., Hammill & Larsen, 1978; Kavale & Mattson, 1983). By contrast, the result of a *summative evaluation* cannot be used to inform instruction because it is conducted after instruction has been completed (e.g., at the end of a grading period or school year).

- See Bushell and Baer (1994) for a powerful argument in support of making direct and frequent measurement of student performance an integral part of educational practice.

- Curriculum-based assessment is a formative evaluation method that measures a student's progress in the actual curriculum in which the student is participating.
- Direct and daily measurement involves assessing a student's performance on a specific skill each time it is taught.
- Precision teaching is a special case of direct and daily measurement in which the Standard Celeration Chart is used to guide instructional decisions based on count per unit of time.

Teaching & Learning in School: Tutoring Joe: Winning with the Precision Teaching Team

- Precision teachers are guided by four basic principles: (1) frequency (a count per unit of time) provides a universal measure of performance; (2) count each time you teach; (3) display student performance on the Standard Celeration Chart to evaluate teaching and learning; and (4) the learner knows best. Precision teaching methods used to improve reading skills were charting 1-minute timed readings, sprinting, segmenting long words, and celebrating accomplishments.

- Direct Instruction is a thoroughly developed model of explicit instruction.
- Content enhancements make instruction more effective for *all* students; their use should not be restricted to students with learning disabilities.

- content enhancement
- mnemonic strategies
- learning strategy

Educational Approaches

- Contemporary "best practice" in educating students with learning disabilities involves approaches such as explicit instruction, content enhancements, and learning strategies.

- If you think that content enhancements such as guided notes are "spoon-feeding" students and making learning too easy, consider this: when students use guided notes, they are actively responding and interacting with the curriculum content. Teachers make it too easy when they allow students to passively attend to ongoing instruction.
- The learning strategies approach does not mean teachers can abandon explicit instruction in basic skills. "If the skills tool box is empty, learning strategies will be ineffective" (Deshler, 1998).

- Direct Instruction programs consist of carefully scripted, field-tested lessons in which students respond, both chorally and individually, to a fast-paced series of learning tasks presented by the teacher. Careful selection and sequencing of tasks in the lessons helps students systematically acquire important background knowledge so they can explicitly apply it and link it to new knowledge.
- Content enhancements, such as graphic organizers, visual displays, guided notes, and mnemonic strategies help make curriculum content more accessible to students with learning disabilities.
- Learning strategies help students guide themselves successfully through specific tasks or general problems.

Teaching & Learning in School: What Is Direct Instruction?

- The Direct Instruction Model (DI) is the most carefully developed and thoroughly tested program for teaching reading, math, writing, spelling and thinking skills to children. Some characteristics of DI are high rates of student engagement, immediate feedback, scripted lessons, and learner-tested curriculum design.

Teaching & Learning in School: Mnemonic Strategies

- Many students with mild cognitive disabilities have difficulty remembering verbal information. A variety of mnemonic strategies (e.g., keyword method, pegword method, letter strategies) can be useful, depending on the type of information that needs to be remembered.

	• During the 1995–1996 school year, 42% of students with learning disabilities were served in the regular classroom (U.S. Department of Education, 1998). • Another strategy for increasing the likelihood of successful inclusion is to find out their secrets for success in a particular teacher's classroom (Monda-Amaya, Dieker, & Reed, 1998). • During the 1995–1996 school year, a resource room was the primary educational placement for 39% of all students with learning disabilities (U.S. Department of Education, 1998). • During the 1995–1996 school year, 17% of students with learning disabilities were served in separate classrooms (U.S. Department of Education, 1998). • Fewer than 1% of students with learning disabilities are served in separate schools (U.S. Department of Education, 1998).
Educational Placement Alternatives	• Most students with learning disabilities spend at least part of each school day in the regular classroom. • In some schools, a consultant teacher helps regular classroom teachers work with children with learning disabilities. • In the resource room, a specially trained teacher works with the children on particular skill deficits for one or more periods per day. • A few children with learning disabilities attend separate classrooms. This placement option, however, should be used only after legitimate attempts to serve the child in a less restrictive setting have failed, and it should not be considered permanent.
Current Issues and Future Trends	• The discussion and debate over what constitutes a true learning disability are likely to continue. It is most important for schools to respond to the individual needs of all children who have difficulty learning. • Most professionals and advocates for students with learning disabilities do not support "full inclusion," which would eliminate the continuum of service delivery options. • Students with learning disabilities possess positive attributes and interests that teachers should identify and try to strengthen.

CHAPTER SEVEN
LEARNING DISABILITIES

Guided Review _____

I. Defining Learning Disabilities
    A. What is the IDEA definition of learning disabilities?

        1. _____

        _____

        _____

    B. The NJCLD Definition
        1. What are weaknesses of the IDEA definition of learning disabilities?

            a) _____

            b) _____

            c) _____

            d) _____

            e) _____

II. Characteristics of Students with Learning Disabilities

    A. What are the three criteria for identifying learning disabilities?

        1. _____

        2. _____

        3. _____

    B. Reading Problems
        1. What has recent research revealed about reading disabilities (Torgesen & Wagner, 1998)?

            a) _____

            b) _____

2. Written Language Deficits
   a) What self-regulation and self-assessment strategies are seldom used by students with learning disabilities?

      1) _____

      2) _____

      3) _____

      4) _____

      5) _____

3. Math Underachievement
   a) Which aspects of mathematics pose major problems to many students with LD?

      1) _____

      2) _____

4. Social Skills Deficits
   a) What are the effects of poor social skills?

      1) _____

      2) _____

      3) _____

      4) _____

C. Attention Problems and Hyperactivity
   1. What is the prevalence of ADHD?

      a) _____

   2. Drug Therapy
      a) What are effects of stimulant medication on children with ADHD (Swanson et al., 1993)?

      1) _____

      2) _____

      3) _____

      4) _____

D. Behavioral Problems
   1. What percentage of students with learning disabilities also have behavior problems?

      a) _____

E. What is the defining characteristic of a learning disability?

    1. _____

      _____

III. Prevalence
    A. What is the prevalence of students with LD?

        1. _____ million children between ages 6 to 21

        2. _____ percent of all school-age children with disabilities

        3. _____ students in the United States have a learning disability

IV. Causes of Learning Disabilities: What are the theories for causes of learning disabilities?
    A. Brain Damage
        1. Why do most special educators place little value on theories linking LD to brain damage?

            a) _____

            b) _____

    B. Heredity
    C. Biochemical Imbalance
        1. Food additives
        2. Vitamins
    D. Environmental Factors
V. Assessment.
    A. Norm-referenced Tests
        1. How are norm-referenced tests designed?

            a) _____

            b) _____

    B. Criterion-referenced Tests
        1. How do criterion-referenced tests differ from norm-referenced tests?

            a) _____

    C. Informal Reading Inventories
    D. Curriculum-based Assessment
        1. Direct daily measurement
            a) What are the advantages of direct daily measurement?

                1) _____

                2) _____

b) What is precision teaching?

   1) _____

   _____

c) What procedures are used by precision teachers?

   1) _____

   2) _____

   3) _____

   4) _____

   5) _____

   6) _____

   7) _____

VI. Educational Approaches
   A. What have researchers recognized about students with disabilities?

   1. _____

   2. _____

   3. _____

   B. Explicit Instruction
      1. Teachers use explicit instruction when they do the following:

      a) _____

      b) _____

      c) _____

      d) _____

      e) _____

   C. Content Enhancements
      1. What are the different types of content enhancements?

      a) _____

      b) _____

      c) _____

D. Learning Strategies
  1. What is a learning strategy?

     a) _____

     _____

VII. Educational Placement Alternatives
  A. Regular Classroom
    1. What model is used by many school districts to facilitate full inclusion?

       a) _____

  B. Consultant Teacher
    1. How do consultant teachers provide support to regular classroom teachers?

       a) _____

       b) _____

    2. What is a major advantage of the consultant model?

       a) _____

  C. Resource Room
    1. What are some advantages to the resource room model?

       a) _____

       b) _____

       c) _____

    2. What are some disadvantages to the resource room model?

       a) _____

       b) _____

       c) _____

VIII. What Are the Current Issues and Future Trends of Learning Disabilities?

  A. _____

  B. _____

  C. _____

     _____

CHAPTER SEVEN
LEARNING DISABILITIES

Objectives_____

1. Explain the three criteria which must be met when identifying students with learning disabilities.

2. Describe the characteristics of students with learning disabilities.

3. Identify the prevalence of students with learning disabilities.

4. Describe the four types of suspected causes of learning disabilities.

5. Explain the assessment process for identifying students with learning disabilities.

6. Discuss the necessity of direct and daily measurement.

7. Describe the following educational approaches: direct instruction, content enhancements, and learning strategies.

8. Explain the various types of service delivery for students with learning disabilities.

9. Discuss the controversy of full inclusion versus maintaining the continuum of services.

Self-check Quiz _____

1. The definition of learning disability includes which of the following?
   a. discrepancy criterion
   b. exclusionary clause
   c. both a & b
   d. none of the above

2. Which of the following describes a reading disability?
   a. Juan, a third grader, experienced letter reversals in the first and second grade. He is now able to appropriately identify all of his letters and reads on grade level.
   b. Jose is unable to read his text books because he has a visual impairment.
   c. Janis has been diagnosed with dyslexia and has had individualized instruction. She is now able to read on grade level with her peers with limited assistance from her teacher.
   d. Jill has been diagnosed with ADHD and will not sit still long enough to read her assignments.

3. The IDEA definition of specific learning disabilities includes:
   a. children who have learning problems which are primarily the result of visual, hearing, or motor disabilities.
   b. individuals who have perceptual disorders, brain injury, minimal brain dysfunction, and developmental aphasia.
   c. individuals who have a disorder in one or more of the basic psychological processes involved in understanding or using written or spoken language which manifests itself in an imperfect ability to listen, think, read, etc.
   d. both b & c

4. Students with learning disabilities often experience difficulty socializing with their peers. Which of the following statements is true?
   a. Three-fourths of students with learning disabilities exhibit social skills deficits.
   b. Most infractions occur on the playground.
   c. Social skills are difficult to assess and teach, so teachers should spend minimal instructional time addressing social skills.
   d. Social skills have little relevance to what a student should be learning in school.

5. Which of the following is either implied or stated in the NJCLD definition of learning disabilities?
   a. An extrinsic factor has interfered with normal development of the child's ability to process information, acquire language skills, or master academic achievement.
   b. An intrinsic factor has interfered with the normal development of the child's ability to process information, acquire language skills, or master academic achievement.
   c. Individuals with learning disabilities have normal information-processing skills.
   d. Individuals with learning disabilities have normal language skills.

6. What percentage of the student population currently has the diagnosis of ADHD?
   a. 1–2%
   b. 20+%
   c. 3–5%
   d. 5–10%

7. Children with learning disabilities are a _____ group.
   a. heterogeneous
   b. homogenous
   c. similar
   d. all of the above

8. What is the current ratio of students with learning disabilities to students without learning disabilities?
   a. 1 of every 100 students
   b. 5 of every 100 students
   c. 10 of every 100 students
   d. 20 of every 100 students

9. Learning disabilities for most children are probably the result of:
   a. brain damage.
   b. heredity.
   c. biochemical imbalance.
   d. none of the above

10. Which of the following best illustrates a student at risk for a learning disability?
    a. Sally has had many books read to her during her development, and her parents regularly talk with her about what is occurring in her environment.
    b. Janet's parents are deaf, but they have a part-time aide who is working with her on language development. Janet can now speak and sign.
    c. Jessica is from an illiterate family, therefore she has had limited experiences with print.
    d. Molly has a physical disability and is in a wheelchair.

11. Indirect assessment measures_____— in contrast to direct assessment which measures _____.
    a. overall academic achievement; specific skills and behaviors students need to be taught
    b. specific skills and behaviors that students need to be taught; overall academic achievement
    c. what to teach; how to teach
    d. how to teach; what to teach

12. Which of the following is an example of direct instruction?
    a. working one-on-one with students
    b. implementing cooperative learning groups
    c. gathering data, modeling step-by-step strategies, providing adequate practice and feedback
    d. assigning 20 math facts to complete every day

13. Guided notes are helpful to the student who:
    a. has difficulty listening.
    b. has language deficits.
    c. has fine motor deficits.
    d. all of the above

14. An instructional approach which teaches students to guide themselves successfully through a learning task is called:
    a. graphic organizers.
    b. precision teaching.
    c. direct instruction.
    d. learning strategies.

15. Which of the following students would most likely be considered for a self-contained classroom?
    a. Michael demonstrates severe defects in math, but for all other subjects his performance is on grade level. He is motivated to learn and attempts to abide by the teacher's recommendations.
    b. Janie has difficulty in reading, which affects her performance in other content areas. In addition, she is highly disorganized, distractible, and physically aggressive with her classmates.
    c. Dominic has a reading disability. He has learned strategies to compensate for this disorder. His performance in most academic areas is satisfactory.
    d. Betty Ann was in a self-contained classroom in elementary school because of significant academic deficits. In middle school, Betty Ann was taught strategies to learn more efficiently, which has drastically improved her academic performance.

CHAPTER EIGHT
EMOTIONAL AND BEHAVIORAL DISORDERS

Focus Questions

- **Why should a child who behaves badly be considered disabled?**

  How a person behaves is one of the most critical factors in determining access to, acceptance, and success in school, work, and the community. Our behavior can also have a direct influence on how well we learn and perform. For example, a student who spends a large part of his day climbing on furniture, making obscene gestures or noises, defying the teacher, and/or touching his classmates is not likely to learn much. The adult who spends part of his day arguing with co-workers or customers, and refusing to work at speed is not likely to get much work done or keep his job. Why then should children who behave badly be considered disabled? Their noxious or withdrawn behaviors can interfere with their acceptance, how well they perform, and ultimately the quality of their lives.

- **Who is more severely disabled: the acting-out, antisocial child or the withdrawn child?**

  Often the real question becomes "Which is more severely 'handicapping' to those who interact with these children?" Acting-out children may be described as over-responsive to their environment—they disrupt the ongoing activities in their classroom, home, or community. Their emotional and behavioral disorder interferes with their acquisition of social and academic skills as well as the activities of those around them. Withdrawn children, on the other hand, may be described as unresponsive to their environment. Although their behavior may not disrupt others to the same degree, the result is the same as with disruptive children: They fail to learn those skills that will provide them with acceptance and access to the same opportunities as other children. From an educational perspective, acting-out and withdrawn children are equally disabled because both encounter problems with the acquisition of academic, social, personal, and vocational skills. From an identification perspective, the withdrawn child may be more disabled because he or she is less likely to be identified to receive treatment.

- **How are behavior problems and academic performance interrelated?**

  When teachers spend much of their day attending to inappropriate student behavior, they do not have time to provide quality instruction. Effective instructional programs increase the likelihood that students will attend to the academic tasks at hand and decrease student opportunities to misbehave. Learning occurs as a result of the interactions between a learner and the learning environment. Given this view of the learning process, any variables that influence the interaction between the student and the classroom activities will consequently affect learning.

- **How can a teacher's efforts to diffuse a classroom disturbance contribute to an escalation of misbehavior?**

  Teachers of students with emotional and behavioral disorders often create an environment in which coercion is the primary means by which students are motivated to participate and follow rules. Coercive environments, in addition to promoting escape and avoidance behavior by those being coerced, do not teach what to do, as much as, they focus on what not to do. Teachers of students with emotional and behavioral disorders must strive to design classroom environments that not only are effective in decreasing antisocial behavior but also increase the frequency of positive teacher-student interactions.

- **What are the most important skills for teachers of students with emotional and behavioral disorders?**

  The most important skills of any teacher, whether in general or special education, are those needed to teach skills to students. Good teaching skills are also necessary for the teacher of children with emotional and behavioral disorders. Managing behavior problems may be the most formidable task facing the teacher of these children, but ultimately he or she is responsible for creating a productive learning environment.

Chapter Overview _____

In the title of one of his books, Nicholas Hobbs (1982) referred to children with emotional and behavioral disorders as "troubled and troubling children." It is easy to see how these children might be "troubled." Many of them have few friends, adults often avoid them, and their family members are often confused and embarrassed by their misbehavior. As you read and study more about these children, or better yet, spend time with them, you will see why Hobbs called them "troubling." Many of them behave in such a persistent noxious manner that they seem to invite negative responses from others.

As with children with learning disabilities and mental retardation, not all children with behavioral disorders are alike. The chapter reviews, in detail, dominant characteristics of this group of exceptional children. The range of behaviors exhibited by these children is discussed, as well as their intellectual ability and academic achievement.

The Council for Children with Behavior Disorders (CCBD) and the National Mental Health and Special Education Coalition have proposed a definition of emotional and behavioral disorders as a disability characterized by "behavioral or emotional responses in school programs so different from appropriate age, cultural, or ethnic norms that they adversely affect educational performance." There are two general types of emotional and behavioral disorders, often referred to as externalizing and internalizing problems. Children with externalizing problems frequently exhibit antisocial behavior; children with internalizing problems are overly withdrawn and lack social skills needed to interact effectively with others.

The suggested causes of emotional and behavioral disorders fall into two general categories: biological and environmental. For the vast majority of these children, it appears that environmental factors have a dominant influence on their behavior. Events in school and at home play an important role in the development of environmentally disordered behavior. The influence of biology is likely to be stronger in children with severe and profound behavioral disorders.

Reviewed in the chapter are several approaches to educating children with behavior disorders. Each has its own definition, purpose of treatment, and intervention. In practice, few programs or teachers use only the techniques suggested by one model. It is evident that effective instructional strategies for children with emotional and behavioral disorders involve teaching social skills, approaches to classroom management, self-management strategies, and group process techniques.

It is important to note that many children with emotional and behavioral disorders given the right learning environment behave in the very same way as nondisabled children for much of the school day. They can be energetic, creative, likable, and fun to be around. For many of these children, it is a "troubled life" that causes them to be both "troubled and troubling." Teachers must work to create a less than troubling learning environment for these children—a task that is easier said than done, but one that is certainly possible and rewarding when accomplished.

CHAPTER EIGHT AT A GLANCE

MAIN TOPICS	KEY POINTS	KEY TERMS	MARGIN NOTES
Defining Emotional and Behavioral Disorders	• There is no single, widely used definition of emotional and behavioral disorders. Most definitions require a child's behavior to differ markedly (extremely) and chronically (over time) from current social or cultural norms. • Many leaders in the field do not like the federal definition of "seriously emotionally disturbed" in IDEA because students who are socially maladjusted are not eligible for special education services. • The CCBD and the NMSEC have proposed a definition of emotional and behavioral disorders as a disability characterized by "behavioral or emotional responses in school programs so different from appropriate age, cultural, or ethnic norms that they adversely affect educational performance."	• serious emotional disturbance • chronicity • severity	• Children without disabilities sometimes act in the same ways as children with emotional and behavioral disorders, but not as often or with such intensity. And, of course, many children with emotional and behavioral disorders are likable. • The NMSEC is a coalition of more than 30 professional mental health and education associations concerned with the education and welfare of children with emotional and behavioral disorders.
Characteristics of Children with Emotional and Behavioral Disorders	• On the average, students with emotional and behavioral disorders score somewhat below normal on IQ tests and achieve academically below what their scores would predict. • Many students with emotional and behavioral disorders have difficulty developing and maintaining interpersonal relationships. • Children with externalizing problems frequently exhibit antisocial behavior; many become delinquents as adolescents.	• externalizing behaviors • internalizing behaviors • response cards	• Students with emotional and behavioral disorders are 13.3 times more likely to be arrested during their school careers than nondisabled students are (Doren, Bullis, & Benz, 1996a), and 58% are arrested within five years of leaving high school (Chesapeake Institute, 1994). • Students with emotional and behavioral disorders who have poor social skills are much more likely to be victims of personal violence, sexual abuse, and other criminal acts during and after their high school careers (Doren, Bullis, & Benz, 1996b).

Topic	Content	
	• Even when IQ scores are taken into account, children with emotional and behavioral disorders achieve below the levels suggested by their scores. • Providing students with frequent response opportunities during instruction increases both on-task behavior and achievement. • To learn how puppetry can help students with emotional and behavioral disorders develop social and affective awareness and social skills, see Caputo (1993). Storytelling can also be an effective means for helping students learn to understand and express their emotions (Bauer & Balius, 1995).	
Teaching & Learning in School: Using Response Cards to Increase Participation and Achievement	• Children with internalizing problems are overly withdrawn and lack social skills needed to interact effectively with others. • When response cards, signs, cards, or items that are simultaneously held up by all students to display their responses to a question presented by the teacher, are used, students have a higher participation rate and score higher on quizzes and tests.	
Prevalence	• Although the U.S. Department of Education has traditionally estimated that children with emotional and behavioral disorders comprise 2% of the school-age population, the number of children served is less than half of the 2% estimate. • The ratio of boys to girls in programs for students with emotional and behavioral disorders is approximately 4:1. Although there are many exceptions, boys are more likely to have externalizing problems, and girls are more likely to have internalizing problems.	• delinquent • recidivist
Causes of Emotional and Behavioral Disorders	• The causes suggested for behavioral disorders are biological and environmental. • Because of its central role in a child's life, the school can also be an important contributing factor to a behavior problem.	• coercive pain control • Child abuse is also correlated with a higher-than-usual incidence of antisocial behavior.

	Key Terms	Summary Points	Additional Points
Identification and Assessment	• screening • multiple-gating screening • projective test • frequency • duration • latency • topography • magnitude • functional assessment	• Although several screening tests have been developed, many school districts do not use any systematic method for identifying children with emotional and behavioral disorders. • Whereas antisocial children stand out, withdrawn children may go unnoticed. • Screening should be conducted as early as possible and include information from multiple agents and settings. • Projective tests are rarely useful in planning and implementing interventions. • Direct and continuous observation and measurement of specific problem behaviors within the classroom is an assessment technique that indicates directly whether and for which behaviors intervention is needed. • Five measurable dimensions of behavior are frequency, duration, latency, topography, and magnitude.	• The primary purpose of initial assessment is not to determine whether the child *has* something called an emotional and behavioral disorder but to see whether the child's behavior *is different enough to warrant special services* and, if so, to indicate what those services should be. • Many districts now require an intermediate step between screening and full-scale assessment. This step consists of interventions designed to maintain the child in the regular classroom and to prevent a suspected or developing problem from getting worse. • The *Early Screening Project* is an adaptation of the SSBD for use with preschool children ages 3 to 5 (Walker, Severson, & Feil, 1994). • IDEA recommends that functional assessments be conducted as part of designing positive behavioral support plans for students with disabilities.
Educational Approaches	• eclectic approach • alterable variables • ecological management • wraparound services • positive reinforcement • shaping • contingency contracting • extinction	• Six conceptual models of children's emotional and behavioral disorders have been proposed: biogenic, psychodynamic, psychoeducational, humanistic, ecological, and behavioral. Although each approach has a distinct theoretical basis and suggests types of treatment, many teachers use techniques from more than one of the models. • Research supports the behavioral and ecological models, which analyze and modify the ways in which a child interacts with the environment.	• In the process of learning how to participate in collaborative learning activities and serving as academic tutors for one another, students with emotional and behavioral disorders may also learn better social and affective skills (Cartledge & Cochran, 1993; Cochran, Feng, Cartledge, & Hamilton, 1993). • Most effective teachers of students with emotional and behavioral disorders are expert at recognizing and using nonverbal cues that are part of every teacher-student interaction.

- differential reinforcement
- response cost
- time out
- overcorrection
- token economy
- proactive strategies
- self-monitoring
- self-evaluation
- peer monitoring
- peer confrontation
- group process
- group-oriented contingencies
- differential acceptance
- empathetic relationship

- Teachers should concentrate their resources and energies on alterable variables- those things in a student's environment that the teacher can influence.
- Many students with emotional and behavioral disorders benefit from systematic social skills training.
- Self-management skills can help students develop a sense of control over their environment, responsibility for their actions, and self-direction.
- A good classroom management system uses proactive strategies to create a positive, supportive, and noncoercive environment that promotes prosocial behavior and academic achievement.
- Group process approaches use the power of the peer group to help students with emotional and behavioral disorders learn to behave appropriately.
- Two important affective traits for teachers of students with emotional and behavioral disorders are differential acceptance and empathetic relationship.

Teaching & Learning in School: "Look, I'm All Finished!" Recruiting Teacher Attention

- Politely recruiting teacher attention and assistance can help students with disabilities function more independently and actively influence their quality of instruction.

Profiles & Perspectives: My Return Voyage

- The power of the peer group can be an effective means of producing positive changes in children with emotional and behavioral disorders.

Educational Placement Alternatives	• Most students with emotional and behavioral disorders are served in self-contained classrooms. • Nearly half of students with emotional and behavioral disorders spend up to half of the school day in regular classrooms. • Comparing the behavioral and academic progress of students with emotional and behavioral disorders in different educational placements in an effort to determine which setting is the best is difficult because students with milder disabilities are included first and more often, whereas those students who exhibit more severe behavioral disturbances tend to remain in special classes.
Current Issues and Future Trends	• Special education services are needed for the many incarcerated adolescents with emotional and behavioral disorders in correctional institutions. • Successful programs for students with emotional and behavioral disorders are characterized by systematic, data-based interventions; continuous assessment and monitoring of student progress; provision for practice of new skills; matching treatment with the problem; multicomponent treatments; programming for transfer and maintenance of newly learned skills; and commitment to follow-up and continued intervention as needed.

CHAPTER EIGHT
EMOTIONAL AND BEHAVIORAL DISORDERS

Guided Review _____

I. Defining Emotional and Behavioral Disorders
    A. Why are emotional and behavioral disorders difficult to define?

        1. _____

        2. _____

        3. _____

        4. _____

    B. How does IDEA define serious emotional disturbance?

        1. _____

            _____

        2. _____

        3. _____

        4. _____

        5. _____

            _____

    C. What three conditions must be met under the IDEA definition of EBD?

        1. _____

        2. _____

        3. _____

    D. CCBD Definition of Emotional or Behavioral Disorders
        1. Behavioral or emotional responses so different from appropriate age, cultural, or ethnic norms they adversely affect educational performance. Such a disability is:

            a) _____

                _____

b) _____

_____

c) _____

2. Emotional and behavior disorders can co-exist with other disabilities.
3. Which children may be included in this category?

   a) _____

   b) _____

   c) _____

   d) _____

II. Characteristics of Children with Emotional and Behavioral Disorders
   A. What are some examples of externalizing behaviors?

   1. _____

   2. _____

   3. _____

   4. _____

   B. What are some examples of internalizing behaviors?

   1. _____

   2. _____

   3. _____

   4. _____

   C. School Achievement and Intelligence
      1. What does the research report about academic outcomes for students with EBD?

      a) _____

      b) _____

      c) _____

      d) _____

   D. Social Skills and Interpersonal Relationships
      1. What does the research report about the social relationships of secondary students with EBD?

      a) _____

b) _____

c) _____

d) _____

III. Prevalence
   A. How many children received special education under the IDEA emotional and behavioral disorders category in the 1996-97 school year?

      1. _____ children between ages 6 to 21

      2. _____ percent of the student population

      3. Only about _____ to _____ percent are being served

   B. What is the male to female ratio of identified students with EBD?

      1. _____

   C. Juvenile Delinquency
      1. Of all violent crimes committed, what percentage are committed by juveniles?

         a) _____

      2. Children under age 15 account for what percentage of all arrests?

         a) _____

      3. About how many juveniles are recidivists?

         a) _____

IV. Causes of Emotional and Behavioral Disorders
   A. What is the relationship between EBD and biological factors?

      1. _____

         _____

      2. _____

         _____

      3. _____

         _____

   B. Environmental Factors
      1. What three primary causal factors contribute to conduct disorders or antisocial behavior (Dodge, 1993)?

         a) _____

b) _____

c) _____

C. The Influence of Home
   1. Antisocial children are more likely to come from homes in which:

   a) _____

   b) _____

   c) _____

   d) _____

   e) _____

D. How does the community influence problem behaviors?

   1. _____

   _____

E. The Influence of School
   1. What schooling practices are likely to contribute to the development of EBD?

   a) _____

   b) _____

   c) _____

   d) _____

   2. A child's behavior pattern at school is the result of a complex interaction of:

   a) _____

   b) _____

   c) _____

V. Identification and Assessment
   A. What four questions should assessment of EBD answer?

   1. _____

   2. _____

   3. _____

   4. _____

B. School-related assessment of children with EBD should include:

1. _____

2. _____

3. _____

4. _____

5. _____

6. _____

C. What are three widely used screening tests for EBD?

1. _____

2. _____

3. _____

D. Projective Tests
    1. What are examples of projective tests?

    a) _____

    b) _____

    c) _____

    2. What are the problems with projective tests?

    a) _____

    b) _____

    c) _____

E. Direct Observation and Measurement of Behavior
    1. What are five measurable dimensions of behavior?

    a) _____

    b) _____

    c) _____

    d) _____

    e) _____

131

2. What is the advantage of assessing and describing behavior in measurable dimensions?

a) _____

_____

F. What is functional assessment?

1. _____

_____

VI. Educational Approaches
   A. Theoretical and Conceptual Models
      1. What are six conceptual models of EBD?

a) _____

b) _____

c) _____

d) _____

e) _____

f) _____

   B. Curriculum Goals
      1. What should be included in special education programs for students with EBD?

a) _____

_____

      2. Why is social skills instruction important?

a) _____

      3. How do children with EBD best learn academic skills?

a) _____

b) _____

   C. Alterable Variables
      1. What are the two primary responsibilities of the special education teacher?

a) _____

b) _____

D. Behavior Management
　　1. Behavioral teaching strategies include:

　　　　a) _____

　　　　b) _____

　　　　c) _____

　　　　d) _____

　　　　e) _____

　　　　f) _____

　　　　g) _____

　　　　h) _____

　　　　i) _____

　　2. Self-management
　　　　a) What is self-monitoring?

　　　　　　1) _____

　　　　b) What is self-evaluation?

　　　　　　1) _____

　　　　c) What are the benefits of self-management?

　　　　　　1) _____

　　　　　　2) _____

　　3. Peer Mediation and Support
　　　　a) What strategies can be used for teaching peers to help one another?

　　　　　　1) _____

　　　　　　2) _____

　　　　　　3) _____

　　　　b) What are group contingencies?

　　　　　　1) _____

E. What are two affective traits of a good teacher?

    1. _____

    2. _____

VII. Educational Placement Alternatives
  A. What are five types of programs for students with EBD in grades 7 to 12?

    1. _____

    2. _____

    3. _____

    4. _____

    5. _____

VIII. Current Issues and Future Trends
  A. What are the current issues in the field of EBD?

    1. _____

    2. _____

    _____

CHAPTER EIGHT
EMOTIONAL AND BEHAVIORAL DISORDERS

Objectives

1. Explain the components that most definitions of emotional and behavioral disorders have in common.

2. Describe the characteristics of children with emotional and behavioral disorders.

3. Define and give examples of internalizing and externalizing behavior problems.

4. Identify the prevalence of students with emotional and behavioral disorders.

5. Identify the two categories of causes of emotional and behavioral disorders.

6. Describe environmental factors that may contribute to problem behaviors.

7. Describe the types of assessment methods used to identify children with emotional and behavioral disorders.

8. Explain which educational approaches have proven to be most effective for students with emotional and behavioral disorders.

9. Describe the two important affective traits teachers must possess to effectively teach children with emotional and behavioral disorders.

10. Describe the educational placement alternatives for children with emotional and behavioral disorders.

Self-check Quiz

1. Which of the following statements about children with behavior disorders is true?
   a. The behavior of children with emotional and behavioral disorders is just as much of an obstacle to functioning and learning as physical and/or developmental disabilities.
   b. The inappropriate behavior of children with emotional and behavioral disorders is similar in intensity to the inappropriate behaviors of children without behavior disorders.
   c. Children with emotional and behavioral disorders make up a small portion of students receiving special education services.
   d. Only children with obnoxious, acting-out, antisocial behaviors are considered to have an emotional or behavioral disorder.

2. Special educators who work with students with severe emotional and behavioral disorders have not reached consensus on a definition because:
   a. disordered behavior is not a social construct.
   b. expectations and norms for appropriate behavior are similar across ethnic groups.
   c. different theories of emotional disturbance use concepts and terminology that do little to promote meaning from one definition to another.
   d. both a & c

3. Under IDEA, to be identified as having an emotional or behavioral disorder, which of the following conditions must be met?
   a. difficulty in school
   b. severity
   c. chronicity
   d. all of the above

4. Which is NOT one of the five types of behavior problems that are specified in the IDEA definition of emotional and behavioral disorders?
   a. pervasive mood of unhappiness
   b. social maladjustment
   c. inappropriate types of behavior under normal circumstances
   d. inability to build and maintain relationships

5. Emotional and behavioral disorders are characterized as:
   a. internalizing behaviors.
   b. externalizing behaviors.
   c. both a & b
   d. none of the above

6. Bradford frequently ignores his teacher, complains, and hits other students. Bradford is engaging in:
   a. adolescent behaviors.
   b. externalizing behaviors.
   c. internalizing behaviors.
   d. schizophrenic behaviors.

7. Without early intervention, a young child who exhibits deviant behavior patterns:
   a. will grow out of those deviant behavior patterns as he gets older.
   b. will probably become a juvenile delinquent.
   c. will probably have the same likelihood of getting arrested as children without emotional and behavioral disorders.
   d. both b & c

8. Which of the following students is most likely to be referred for screening for emotional or behavioral disorders?
   a. Frank, a child who does not complete assignments and frequently falls asleep in class
   b. Amy, who frequently complains of stomach aches and goes into stages of deep depression
   c. Antonia, who is extremely shy and does not interact with other children
   d. Brian, who does not comply with the class rules and uses profanity toward his teacher

9. What percentage of students with emotional and behavioral disorders are receiving special education services based on the 1997 federal report?
   a. 20-30%
   b. 40-50%
   c. 60-70%
   d. 100%

10. Which of the following statements regarding juvenile delinquents is true?
    a. Juveniles commit about 10% of all violent crimes.
    b. Recidivists are likely to begin their criminal careers by about age 12.
    c. About 50% of juvenile delinquents are recidivists.
    d. both b & c

11. Which is NOT an example of a proactive strategy?
    a. immediately enforcing the consequences when a student misbehaves
    b. peer mediation and support
    c. teaching self-management skills
    d. establishing clear rules and expectations

12. Most children with emotional and behavioral disorders score:
    a. above normal on IQ tests and academically achieve below what their scores indicate.
    b. in the average range on IQ tests and academically achieve at their grade level.
    c. below normal on IQ tests and academically achieve below what their test scores predict.
    d. below normal on IQ tests and academically achieve above what their test scores predict.

13. Which assessment technique is the least useful in planning and implementing interventions?
    a. screening tests
    b. projective tests
    c. direct observation and measurement of behavior
    d. functional assessment

14. Which conceptual model for emotional and behavioral disorders has been empirically validated as the most effective?
    a. behavioral
    b. psychodynamic
    c. humanistic
    d. ecological

15. Which of the following strategies can best help students with emotional and behavioral disorders develop a sense of control over their environment, responsibility for their actions, and self-direction?
    a. group process
    b. peer mediation
    c. self-management
    d. ecological management

CHAPTER NINE
COMMUNICATION DISORDERS

Focus Questions

- **How can a true communication disorder be differentiated from a communication difference?**

Communication affects the way we learn, our social acceptance and competence, our self-esteem, and our employment opportunities. Yet no two of us communicate in exactly the same way. Communication differences are of little concern so long as they do not impair our ability to express or receive speech and language. Social, cultural, educational, and geographic variables contribute to the communication differences all of us exhibit. When a communication difference is so pronounced, however, that it has an adverse effect on a student's academic achievement in school or interactions with his or her peers, it becomes a handicapping communication disorder.

- **How can a teacher use what is known about typical language development to support children with language impairments?**

Despite the complexity of our language system, most children learn to understand and then to speak during the first few years of life without any formal instruction. Children's abilities and early environments vary widely, but most children follow a relatively predictable sequence in development of speech and language. Understanding how young, normally developing children acquire language is helpful to the teacher or specialist working with children who have delayed or disordered communication. Knowledge of normal language development can help the specialist determine whether a particular child is simply developing language at a slower-than-normal rate or whether the child shows an abnormal pattern of language development.

- **What are the most important functions of an alternative and augmentative communication system?**

Augmentative and alternative communication refers to a diverse set of strategies and methods to assist individuals who are unable to meet their communication needs through speech or writing. The three components of AAC are: a representational symbol set (individually selected vocabulary represented by symbols such as those included in Picture Communication Symbols, Pictogram Ideagram Communication, or Blissymbolics); a means for selecting symbols (e.g., direct selection, scanning, or encoding responses), and a means for transmitting symbols (e.g., a communication board, Prentke Romich Liberator, or DECtalk).

- **What are common elements of effective interventions for speech disorders?**

There are four models used to treat speech disorders: the discrimination model emphasizes the child's ability to detect differences in sound; the phonologic model seeks to identify the patterns of sound production and produce gradually more acceptable sounds; the sensorimotor model emphasizes the motor skills involved in articulation; and the operant conditioning model seeks to shape articulatory responses by providing reinforcing consequences. Although these teaching approaches are very different, they all utilize systematic intervention to correct or improve the impairment. The common elements of effective intervention include providing a good language model, reinforcing the child's improved performance, and encouraging the child to talk.

- **Why are naturalistic interventions more likely to result in maintenance and generalization of a child's new speech and language skills?**

Naturalistic interventions occur in real or simulated activities that naturally occur in the home, school, or community environments in which a child normally functions. Naturalistic interventions (also known as *milieu* teaching strategies) are characterized by their use of dispersed learning trials, attempts to base teaching on the child's attentional lead with the context of normal conversational interchanges, and orientation toward teaching the form and content of language in the context of normal use. Naturalistic approaches are more likely to promote generalization of language skills because instruction occurs in the context of the child's normal daily interactions. This eliminates the step of having to carry over skills learned in didactic contrived situations to natural situations.

Chapter Overview

This chapter focuses on the importance of speech and language in the educational process. Disorders involving students' articulation, voice quality, fluency, and use and understanding of language can significantly influence their learning. Children can have serious difficulties in acquiring the skills they are expected to learn in school if their communication skills are deficient. Because communication is necessary in nearly every aspect of a child's day-to-day routine, its role in learning social and academic skills is critical.

Normal language development follows a relatively predictable sequence. Most children learn to use language without direct instruction; by the time they enter first grade, their grammar and speech patterns match those of the adults around them. When a child's language development deviates from the norm to such an extent that he or she has serious difficulties in learning and in interpersonal relations, the child is said to have a communication disorder. Special education is needed when a communication disorder adversely affects educational performance.

As many as 5% of school-age children have speech impairments serious enough to warrant attention. Nearly twice as many boys as girls have speech impairments. Children with articulation problems represent the largest category of speech-language impairments.

Like most disabilities, communication disorders can have a variety of causes. Communication disorders that are organic are attributed to a specific physical cause. Most communication disorders, however, do not have a known physical origin. Environmental influences, such as the child's opportunity to learn speech and language, are thought to be the major causes of many communication disorders.

Most speech and language assessments today are conducted in the natural settings where the child ordinarily communicates. This is a significant change from the days when most testing was done in clinical settings. A major responsibility of special education is to teach skills that the child can use outside the special education classroom. Assessing the child in those settings and situations where communication is necessary increases the likelihood that meaningful communication skills will be selected for treatment.

There are various treatment approaches to speech and language disorders. With few exceptions, however, treatment of children with such disorders involves aspects of their environment where they need to communicate. The goal of most treatment programs is to teach children to communicate with a variety of other individuals and across a variety of circumstances. Maintaining children in the regular classroom is an important part of achieving this goal.

Augmentative and alternative communication (AAC) may be necessary in severe situations. An augmentative communication system is designed to supplement and enhance a person's communication capabilities.

CHAPTER NINE AT A GLANCE

MAIN TOPICS	KEY POINTS	KEY TERMS	MARGIN NOTES
Communication, Language, and Speech	• Communication is any interaction that transmits information. Narrating, explaining, informing, and expressing are major communicative functions. • A language is an arbitrary symbol system that enables a group of people to communicate; each language has rules of phonology, morphology, syntax, and semantics that describe how users put sound together to convey meaning. • Speech is the vocal response mode of language and the basis on which language develops. • Normal language development follows a relatively predictable sequence. Most children learn to use language without direct instruction, and by the time most children enter first grade, their grammar and speech patterns match those of the adults around them.	• communication • paralinguistic behaviors • nonlinguistic behaviors • kinesics • language • phonology • phonemes • morphology • morpheme • syntax • semantics • pragmatics • speech • respiration • phonation • resonation • articulation • graphemes	• The study of nonlinguistic behaviors that augment language is called **kinesics.** • Phonemes are represented by letters or other symbols between slashes. • The pragmatic model can be helpful in understanding and treating a child's communication disorder. • American Sign Language is a visual-spatial language. • Children with hearing impairments have a special set of problems in learning language. • Children whose expressive vocabularies consist of fewer than 50 words and/or produce limited word combinations at 24 months of age are considered late talkers.
Defining Communication Disorders	• A child has a speech disorder if his or her speech draws unfavorable attention to itself, interferes with the ability to communicate, or causes social or interpersonal problems. • Some children have trouble understanding language (receptive language disorders); others have trouble using language to communicate (expressive language disorders); still others have language delays.	• impaired speech • impaired language • receptive language disorder • expressive language disorder • dialects	• The three basic types of speech disorders are articulation, voice, and fluency. • Language is so important to academic performance that it can be impossible to differentiate a learning disability from a language disorder (Wallach & Butler, 1994). Again, the emphasis should be on remediating a child's skill deficits rather than on labeling them.

	• For children whose native language is not English, the distinction between a language difference and a communication disorder is critical (Roseberry-McKibbin, 1995).	• ASHA estimates that speech, language, and related disorders affect 14 million Americans.	• *Dysarthria* and *apraxia* refer to two groups of articulation disorders caused by neuromuscular impairments. Lack of precise motor control needed to produce and sequence sounds causes distorted and repeated sounds. • Some professionals view learning disabilities and autism primarily as language disorders.
			• organic speech impairments • functional communication disorder • articulation disorders • dysarthria • apraxia • fluency disorder • cluttering • stuttering • voice disorder
Teaching & Learning in School: Leadership Roles Encourage Language in the Classroom	• Speech or language differences based on cultural dialects are not communication disorders; however, children with dialects may also have speech or language disorders. • Teachers can help children develop language skills by encouraging them to assume leadership roles in the classroom. Activities that carry responsibility, power, and prestige are useful in promoting language and social interaction.		
Prevalence	• As many as 5% of school-age children may have speech impairments serious enough to warrant attention. • Nearly twice as many boys as girls have speech impairments. • Children with articulation problems represent the largest category of speech-language impairments.		
Types and Causes of Communication Disorders	• Although some speech disorders have physical (organic) causes, most are functional disorders that cannot be directly attributed to physical conditions. • Types of communication disorders include articulation, voice, fluency, and language disorders. • Stuttering is the most common fluency disorder.		

141

	Key Terms	Key Points
	• dysphonia • phonation disorder • resonance disorder • hypernasality • hyponasality • denasality • aphasia	• *Audiometry* is a formal procedure for testing hearing. • Hadley (1998) describes two procedures for obtaining language samples of young children: a conversational interview and a story re-telling/generating procedure. • McCormick and Schiefelbusch (1990) note the importance of gathering data on both the child's and the adult's behavior in the language interaction. The extent to which the child learns and uses language effectively in the classroom depends to a large extent on the teacher's language behavior.
Identification and Assessment	• audiometry • arena assessment	• Assessment of a suspected communication disorder may include some or all of the following components: case history, physical examination, articulation test, hearing test, auditory discrimination test, language development test, overall language test, conversation with the child or language sample, behavioral observations of child's language competence in social context.
Educational Approaches	• discrimination model • phonological model • sensorimotor model • operant conditioning model • naturalistic interventions • milieu teaching	• Visi-pitch is an example of a visual speech display. It can be used with Apple and IBM computers. • The different types of communication disorders call for different approaches to remediation; behavioral approaches are frequently used. • Articulation disorders may be treated by one of four common models: the discrimination model, the phonological model, the sensorimotor model, or the operant conditioning model.

Teaching & Learning in School: Helping the Child Who Stutters in the Classroom	• Voice disorders can sometimes be treated medically or surgically if there is an organic cause, but the most common remediation is direct vocal rehabilitation. • Treatment of fluency disorders emphasizes either symptom modification or fluency reinforcement. • Language disorders are treated by either individual or group approaches. • Teachers can significantly help a child who stutters by providing a good speech model, improving the child's self-esteem, and creating a good speech environment.
Teaching & Learning in School: Active Learning Dialogues for Students with Language Learning Disabilities	• All classroom teaching and learning consists of dialogue between teachers (or speech-language pathologists) and students. Active learning dialogues have shared social interactional features that build active learning contexts, such as (1) integrating primary sources of information and good literature into curriculum/intervention activities; (2) viewing students as critical thinkers; (3) using dialogues that promote instructional conversations; and (4) supporting student collaboration.

Topic	Key Terms	Summary and Notes
Augmentative and Alternative Communication	• augmentative and alternative communication (AAC) • symbol sets • symbol systems • communication board	• Alternative and augmentative communication (AAC) may be necessary in severe situations. AAC may be unaided or aided and consists of three components: a representational symbol set or vocabulary, a means for selecting the symbols, and a means for transmitting the symbols. • The Crestwood Company publishes a catalog of AAC devices for children and adults. Parette and Angelo (1996) suggest 20 questions that should be asked to assess the impact of AAC on the family.
Profiles & Perspectives: My Communication System		• Using a computer system allows Stephen Hawking, Lucasian Professor of Mathematics and Theoretical Physics at The University of Cambridge, to communicate more effectively.
Educational Service Alternatives		• Most children with speech and language problems attend regular classes. • ASHA can provide further information about the training, qualifications, and responsibilities of speech-language pathologists.
Current Issues and Future Trends		• In the future, communication disorders specialists will probably provide largely consultative services and inservice training. They will help train parents, teachers, and paraprofessionals to work with most children, while they concentrate on diagnosis, programming, and direct intensive services to a few children with special needs. • Further service needs to be directed toward older youths and adults with untreated speech and language problems.

- Use of special devices to help individuals with communication disorders will expand. Electronic devices are now widely used to analyze children's speech and language and to provide instruction.
- Efforts to develop and implement across-the-day interventions programs for children with communication disorders will increase

Teaching & Learning in School: Communication Partners: Strategies for Opening Doors to Communication

- Strategies that communication partners can use that will help individuals with severe speech impairments enjoy increased communication effectiveness are: (1) establish and use fundamental signals; (2) provide opportunities for initiation; (3) present a range of choices and repeat them one at a time; (4) wait for the expression and expansion of ideas; (5) narrow the options to find the category about which the person has something to say; (6) clarify and verify to assure that messages are received correctly; (7) talk "up to" not "down to" the person; (8) recognize deadlocks; and (9) teach these strategies to other partners.

CHAPTER NINE
COMMUNICATION DISORDERS

Guided Review _____

I. Communication, Language, and Speech
   A. Communication
      1. What three elements must occur for an interaction to qualify as communication?

         a) _____

         b) _____

         c) _____

      2. What are three functions of communication?

         a) _____

         b) _____

         c) _____

   B. Language
      1. What is language?

         a) _____

            _____

      2. What are the five dimensions of language?

         a) _____

         b) _____

         c) _____

         d) _____

         e) _____

C. Speech
   1. What is speech?

      a) _____

      _____

   2. What are the four separate, but related processes that produce speech?

      a) _____

      b) _____

      c) _____

      d) _____

D. Normal Language Development
   1. What three aspects of language are integrated to communicate?

      a) _____

      b) _____

      c) _____

   2. How does understanding normal language development help professionals?

      a) _____

      _____

II. Defining Communication Disorders
   A. When is difference considered a disability?

      1. _____

      2. _____

      3. _____

      4. _____

      5. _____

      6. _____

   B. What are speech disorders? A child's speech is considered impaired when it deviates so far from others that it:

      1. _____

      2. _____

3. _____

C. What are language disorders?
   1. What is a receptive language disorder?

      a) _____

   2. What is an expressive language disorder?

      a) _____

   3. ASHA (1993) defines a language disorder as " impaired comprehension and/or use of spoken, written and/or other symbol systems which may involve:

      a) _____

      b) _____

      c) _____

   4. Dialects and Differences
      a) What is a dialect?

         1) _____

            _____

      b) Why must specialists distinguish between dialect and communicative disorders?

         1) _____

            _____

III. Prevalence
   A. In the 1996-97 school year, how many students received special education services under the category of speech or language impairments?

      1. _____ children between ages 6 to 21

      2. _____ percent of the resident population

      3. _____ percent of all students receiving special education services

   B. Why are there differences in prevalence data of children with speech and language disorders?

      1. _____

      2. _____

         _____

IV. Types and Causes of Communication Disorders
   A. What is an organic speech impairment?

       1. _____

       2. What are examples of physical factors that result in language disorders?

           a) _____

           b) _____

           c) _____

           d) _____

           e) _____

           f) _____

       3. What is a functional communication disorder?

           a) _____

   B. Articulation Disorders
       1. What are the four kinds of articulation disorders?

           a) _____

           b) _____

           c) _____

           d) _____

       2. When is a severe articulation disorder present?

           a) _____

               _____

   C. Fluency Disorders
       1. How does ASHA define a fluency disorder?

           a) _____

               _____

       2. What are two types of fluency disorders?

           a) _____

           b) _____

3. What is the cause of stuttering?

   a) _____

4. What is the prevalence of stuttering?

   a) _____

5. In what situations is a child with a fluency disorder likely to stutter?

   a) _____

   b) _____

D. Voice Disorders
   1. How does ASHA define a voice disorder?

      a) _____

   2. What are two basic types of voice disorders?

      a) _____

      b) _____

         1) What are two types of resonance disorders?

            a. _____

            b. _____

E. Language Disorders
   1. How are language disorders classified?

      a) _____

      b) _____

   2. What factors contribute to spoken language disorders?

      a) _____

      b) _____

      c) _____

      d) _____

      e) _____

3. What is aphasia?

    a) _____

        _____

V. Identification and Assessment
    A. What does the development of a case history involve?

        1. _____

        2. _____

        3. _____

        4. _____

        5. _____

    B. What components would a comprehensive evaluation include?

        1. _____

        2. _____

        3. _____

        4. _____

        5. _____

    C. What is an arena assessment?

        1. _____

        2. What are five advantages of an arena assessment?

            a) _____

            b) _____

            c) _____

            d) _____

            e) _____

VI. Educational Approaches
    A. What are the four models for treating articulation disorders?

        1. _____

        2. _____

3. _____

4. _____

B. What are some current methods used to treat stuttering?

1. _____

2. _____

3. _____

4. _____

C. How are different voice disorders treated?

1. _____

2. _____

3. _____

4. _____

D. Treating Language Disorders

1. What are naturalistic interventions/milieu teaching strategies?

a) _____

2. What are three recommendations for using milieu teaching strategies?

a) _____

b) _____

c) _____

VII. Augmentative and Alternative Communication
A. What are three components of ACC?

1. _____

2. _____

3. _____

B. Each component of ACC may be:

1. _____

2. _____

C. Symbol Sets and Symbol Systems
  1. What factors should be considered when choosing an augmentative vocabulary?

      a) _____

      b) _____

      c) _____

D. What are three ways symbols can be selected?

  1. _____

  2. _____

  3. _____

E. What tools may be used for transmitting symbols?

  1. _____

  2. _____

VIII. Educational Service Alternatives
  A. How are most children with speech and language impairments served?

  1. _____

  B. What are some alternatives to the pullout approach?

  1. _____

  2. _____

  C. What is the most prevalent setting for students with communication disorders?

  1. _____

  E. What is the changing role of the communication disorders specialist?

  1. _____

IX. Current Issues and Future Trends

  A. How are the populations of students with communications disorders changing?

  1. _____

  B. What are the across-the-day interventions?

  1. _____

  _____

CHAPTER NINE
COMMUNICATION DISORDERS

Objectives_____

1. Define *communication, language,* and *speech*.

2. Explain the defining features of communication disorders.

3. Distinguish between expressive and receptive communication disorders.

4. Identify the prevalence of children with speech impairments.

5. Describe the causes of communication disorders.

6. Define *articulation, voice, fluency,* and *language disorders*.

7. List and describe the components of language assessment.

8. Describe the educational approaches for treating the various types of language disorders.

9. Define *augmentative* and *alternative communication*, and describe the three components.

10. Describe the various educational service alternatives for children with speech and language problems.

Self-check Quiz _____

1. _____ is a common system used by a group of people for giving meaning to sounds, words, gestures, and other symbols.
   a. Communication
   b. Language
   c. Speech
   d. Paralinguistic behavior

2. _____ is the dimension of language that governs how the basic units of meaning are combined into words.
   a. Phonology
   b. Semantics
   c. Pragmatics
   d. Morphology

3. Which of the following statements is true?
    a. Most children follow a relatively predictable sequence of speech and language development.
    b. The ages at which a normal child develops language are rigid and inflexible.
    c. Knowledge of normal language development is not helpful to specialists.
    d. none of the above

4. A communication difference is a disorder when:
    a. the person is placed at an economic disadvantage.
    b. the transmission and/or perception of messages is faulty.
    c. the problem causes physical damage.
    d. all of the above

5. Yolanda has difficulty following a short series of directions. Which kind of language disorder does she probably have?
    a. receptive
    b. expressive
    c. both expressive and receptive
    d. neither expressive nor receptive

6. What percentage of all students receiving special education services are served under the category of "speech or language impairments"?
    a. 2.3%
    b. 4.1%
    c. 15.7%
    d. 21.6%

7. The percentage of children with speech and language disorders:
    a. decreases significantly from earlier to later grades.
    b. increases significantly from earlier to later grades.
    c. decreases slightly from earlier to later grades.
    d. remains constant throughout earlier and later grades.

8. Francine, a fourth grader, says "wock" when attempting to say "rock," and "wabbit" when attempting to say "rabbit." What kind of articulation disorder does she have?
    a. distortion
    b. substitution
    c. omission
    d. addition

9. Stuttering is a type of:
    a. articulation disorder.
    b. voice disorder.
    c. fluency disorder.
    d. receptive disorder.

10. Which of the following statements is NOT true about stuttering?
    a. People who stutter are fluent about 95% of the time.
    b. Stuttering appears to be related to the setting or circumstances of speech.
    c. The prevalence of stuttering is about 1% of the population regardless of the language spoken.
    d. Stuttering is more commonly reported among adults than children.

11. When Tyrone speaks, he sounds as if his nasal passages are congested. What kind of voice disorder does Tyrone have?
    a. resonance
    b. phonation
    c. articulation
    d. fluency

12. Which of the following is NOT a possible contributing factor to spoken language disorders?
    a. cognitive limitations
    b. hearing impairments
    c. environmental influences
    d. none of the above

13. The _____ model for treating articulation disorders emphasizes developing the child's ability to listen carefully and detect differences between similar sounds.
    a. discrimination
    b. phonologic
    c. sensorimotor
    d. operant conditioning

14. Milieu teaching strategies should be:
    a. lengthy, but positive.
    b. carried out in the natural environment as teaching opportunities occur.
    c. occasioned by teacher interest in the topic.
    d. all of the above

15. Which of the following is NOT a component of the augmentative and alternative communication model?
    a. a means for selecting symbols
    b. a means for transmitting symbols
    c. a means for creating symbols
    d. a representational symbol set or vocabulary

CHAPTER TEN
HEARING LOSS

Focus Questions

- **In what important ways do the child who is deaf and the child who is hard of hearing differ?**

Children who are deaf may be able to perceive some sound but are unable to use their hearing to understand speech. Deaf children develop speech and language skills mainly through their sense of sight. Children who are hard of hearing, on the other hand, have a significant hearing loss that makes special adaptations necessary. It is possible, however, for these children to respond to speech and other auditory stimuli. Children who are hard of hearing develop their speech and language skills mainly through the sense of hearing.

- **Why can reading not simply replace hearing speech as a means of learning and understanding language?**

Years before children learn through reading, hearing is used to acquire information and develop expressive and receptive language skills. By the time typical hearing children enter school, they have a vocabulary of over 5,000 words and have already had 100 million meaningful contacts with language. Even after children learn to read, a good deal of what they learn is acquired through auditory means. Children who learn only through reading would miss out on many critical opportunities to learn and to develop basic communication skills.

- **How do members of the Deaf culture view hearing loss?**

As discussed earlier in the text, a disability may be a handicap in one environment but not in another. There may be no condition for which this is more true than a hearing impairment. When answering this question, it may be helpful to consider another question, "Is it 'nature' that attaches enormous importance to hearing in human development and learning, or is it society?" Most people live in a world where hearing is vital to virtually every aspect of their lives. Yet, there exists a "Deaf culture" that insists it is not a disability to be hearing impaired.

- **How do advocates of oral/aural, total communication, and bilingual-bicultural approaches to educating students who are deaf differ in philosophies and teaching methods?**

The fundamental disagreement concerns the extent to which children who are deaf should express themselves through speech and perceive the communication of others through speechreading and residual hearing. Educators who primarily utilize the oral approach emphasize the development of speech and language and view speech as essential for integration into the hearing world; they often discourage the use of sign language and other gestures. Educators who utilize a total communication approach (i.e., use of sign language, gestures, cues, fingerspelling, and other manual means used along with speech) believe this to be a more natural way of communicating, and believe that this approach enables children who are hearing impaired to more fully express themselves and understand the communication of others.

- **Why do you think American Sign Language (ASL) has not been fully accepted as the language of instruction in school programs for deaf children?**

  American Sign Language (ASL) is structured to accommodate individuals who are hearing impaired, not individuals with hearing. Because ASL has its own vocabulary, syntax, and grammatical rules, it does not correspond exactly to spoken or written English. This makes precise word-for-word translations between ASL and English just as difficult as word-for-word translations between different spoken languages. Many educators fail to see that ASL is a language in its own right, not a manual communication of English.

Chapter Overview

Hearing impairments are usually viewed as one of the more significant disabilities, perhaps because so much of our learning comes to us through the sense of hearing. How many of the debilitating effects associated with hearing impairment stem from the fact that society is designed for hearing individuals? Is hearing impairment the most culturally imposed handicapping condition? This chapter attempts to respond to some of these questions and to remove some of the mystery surrounding individuals with impaired hearing. Also several interesting discussions of the sometimes ethnocentric misunderstanding of deafness and of society's oppression of individuals with hearing impairments are presented.

As with other disabilities, there is no absolute determination of what constitutes impaired hearing. Although children who are deaf are not able to use their hearing to understand speech, they may perceive some sounds. Even with a hearing aid, however, the hearing loss of deaf children is too great to allow them to understand speech through the ears alone. Children who are hard of hearing also have a significant hearing loss, but, unlike deaf children, they can respond to speech and other auditory stimuli. Children who are hard of hearing with the help of hearing aids use their hearing to understand speech. Their speech and language skills, though they may be delayed or deficient, are developed mainly through their sense of hearing.

For many years educators have debated the most appropriate instructional methods for these children. The fundamental disagreement concerns the extent to which children with impaired hearing should express themselves through speech and perceive communication of others through speechreading and residual hearing. Educational programs with an oral emphasis view speech as essential for integration into the hearing world. Much attention is given to amplification, auditory training, speechreading, and the use of technological aids. Other educators utilize a total communication approach with students with impaired hearing. This approach uses a variety of methods to assist the child in expressing, receiving, and developing language. Practitioners of total communication combine sign language and fingerspelling with speech, and their students learn to speak and sign simultaneously. The total communication approach is the predominant method of instruction in schools for students with hearing impairments.

The debate over communication and instructional methods for students with impaired hearing is likely to continue for research has yet to provide a definitive answer to the question of which communication method is best. Fortunately, technological advances are improving the communication abilities of many individuals with hearing impairments, and future technological advances may enable educators to analyze and track their language development with much greater precision. This information could be used to design more appropriate language instruction.

Improvements in technology, continued research on instructional methodology, increased public awareness of the rights of individuals with hearing impairments, and increased acceptance of the use of sign language have positively affected the education, employment, and economic opportunities of children and adults with impaired hearing. It may be that in the not too distant future a hearing impairment will not be a handicapping condition, even in a predominantly hearing world.

CHAPTER TEN AT A GLANCE

MAIN TOPICS	KEY POINTS	KEY TERMS	MARGIN NOTES
Defining Hearing Loss	• Hearing loss exists on a continuum from mild to profound, and most special educators distinguish between children who are deaf and those who are hard of hearing. A deaf child is not able to understand speech through the ears alone. A hard of hearing child is able to use hearing to understand speech, generally with the help of a hearing aid. • Sound is measured by its intensity (decibels [dB]) and frequency (Hertz [Hz]); both dimensions are important in considering the special education needs of a child with a hearing loss. The frequencies most important for understanding speech are 500 to 2,000 Hz.	• deaf • residual hearing • hard of hearing • audition • auricle • auditory canal • decibels • tympanic membrane (eardrum) • ossicles • cochlea • audiometric zero • hertz (Hz)	• The typical hearing child enters school with a vocabulary of more than 5,000 words, the product of perhaps 100 million meaningful contacts with language (Napierkowski, 1981). • Hans Furth (1973), a psychologist who devoted much of his career to studying the language development of people with hearing loss, suggests that a good way to approximate the experience of a child who is deaf from birth or early childhood is to watch a television program in which a foreign language is being spoken—with the sound on the TV set turned off. You would face the double problem of being unable to read lips and understand an unfamiliar language. • Many deaf persons do not view their hearing loss as a disability and consider terms such as *hearing impairment* inappropriate because they suggest a deficiency or pathology. They prefer disability-first terms, such as *teacher of the deaf, school for the deaf,* and *Deaf person.* Like other cultural groups, these members of the Deaf community (who themselves spell *Deaf* with a capital *D*) share a common language and social practices. • A person without external ears could still hear quite well, losing perhaps only 5 to 7 decibels in sound volume. The intensity or loudness of sound is measured in **decibels (dB)**. • Also within the inner ear is the *vestibular mechanism*, which controls the sense of balance by movement-sensitive fluid in the semicircular canals. • *Decibel*, the unit of measure for the intensity of sound, is named for Alexander Graham Bell.

		• A hearing loss of only 15 dB may negatively affect a child's learning to read because some speech sounds are missed (Schirmer, 1998).
		• Of the deaf and hard of hearing children served in special education programs, 95% have a prelinguistic hearing loss (Commission on Education of the Deaf, 1988). • Each year, new cases of hearing loss caused by rubella are recorded. All women of childbearing age should receive the vaccine. • Hearing loss occurs at a higher-than-usual incidence rate among certain groups of individuals with other disabilities. Down syndrome often involves irregularities in the auditory canal and a tendency for fluid to accumulate in the middle ear; as many as 75% of children with Down syndrome may also have significant hearing loss (Nothern & Lemme, 1982). There is also a substantially higher-than-normal incidence of hearing loss among children with cerebral palsy. A hearing test should be part of the assessment of any child who is referred for special education services.
Prevalence	• Students with hearing loss represent about 1.3% of all school-age students receiving special education services. • A national survey of early intervention programs serving children with hearing loss reported that 46% of the children served by the programs were deaf and 54% were hard of hearing.	
Types and Causes of Hearing Loss	• Hearing loss is described as conductive (outer or middle ear) or sensorineural (inner ear) and unilateral (in one ear) or bilateral (in both ears). • A prelingual hearing loss occurs before the child has developed speech and language; a postlingual hearing loss occurs after that time. • Causes of prelingual hearing loss include maternal rubella, heredity, prematurity and complications of pregnancy, and congenital cytomegalovirus (CMV). • Causes of postlingual hearing loss include meningitis, otitis media, and excessive noise.	• conductive hearing loss • sensorineural hearing loss • mixed hearing loss • unilateral • bilateral • congenital • adventitious • prelingual hearing loss • postlingual hearing loss • otitis media

160

Topic	Content	
Identification and Assessment	• A formal hearing test generates an audiogram, which graphically shows the intensity of the faintest sound an individual can hear 50% of the time at various frequencies. • Hearing loss is classified as slight, mild, moderate, severe, or profound, depending on the degree of hearing loss.	• pure-tone audiometry • audiometer • audiogram • speech audiometry • speech reception threshold (SRT) • play audiometry • operant conditioning audiometry • behavior observation audiometry • evoked-response audiometry • impedance audiometry
Profiles & Perspectives: Deaf President Now!	• Gallaudet is a university recognized and respected for its leadership in educating the deaf. Students protested until a deaf person was appointed president. This was referred to as "the deaf civil rights movement." Eventually, Dr. I. King Jordan, a deaf man, was appointed president of Gallaudet.	
Effects of Hearing Loss	• Deaf and hard of hearing students leave high school lagging far behind their hearing peers in English literacy and academic achievement. • Deaf children—especially those with a prelinguistic loss of 90 dB or greater—are at a great disadvantage in acquiring English language skills. • Many deaf individuals choose membership in the deaf community and culture.	• *Deaf of Deaf* is the term used in the Deaf community to refer to children who are deaf with deaf parents. • The correlation between poor reading skills and classroom behavior problems is not limited to students with hearing loss.
Teaching & Learning: Writer's Workshop: Teaching Process Writing to Students Who Are Deaf	• Writer's Workshop is a teaching model based on the principles of teaching the writing process. It has worked successfully with students who are deaf in kindergarten through high school.	

	Description	Key Terms	Notes
Educational Approaches	• The oral/aural approach views speech as essential if students are to function in the hearing world; much emphasis is given to amplification, auditory training, speechreading, the use of technological aids, and above all, talking. • Total communication uses speech and simultaneous manual communication via signs and fingerspelling in English word order. • In the bilingual-bicultural approach, deafness is viewed as a cultural and linguistic difference, not a disability, and ASL is used as the language of instruction.	• cued speech • total communication • fingerspelling	• Roy Holcomb, a deaf graduate of the Texas School for the Deaf and Gallaudet University, coined the term and is credited as the father of total communication (Gannon, 1981). • Fingerspelling is also used by many people who are both deaf and visually impaired. The manual alphabet can be used at close distances or felt with the hand if a person is totally blind.
Assistive Listening Devices and Other Support Technologies	• Amplification and auditory training seek to enable students with hearing loss to use their residual hearing more effectively. • Speechreading can provide useful visual information but has many limitations. Most English sounds cannot be distinguished through vision alone. • An educational interpreter can help some deaf students participate successfully in the regular classroom. • Other support technologies used by persons who are deaf or hard of hearing include text telephones, closed television captioning, and a variety of alerting devices.	• auditory training • auditory learning • speechreading • interpreting • educational interpreter • real-time translation	• Teachers should check daily to see that a child's hearing aid is functioning properly. The Ling Five Sound Test is a quick and easy way to determine whether a child can detect the basic speech sounds (Ling, 1976). With the child's back to the teacher (to ensure that visual clues do not confound the results), the child repeats each of five sounds spoken by the teacher: /a/, /oo/, /e/, /sh/, and /s/. Ling states that these five sounds are representative of the speech energy in every English phoneme and that a child who can detect these five sounds should be able to detect every English speech sound. • Ho (1991) describes the Easy Listener Freefield Sound System, which functions as a specialized portable PA system to increase auditory attention for all students, and the Easy Listener Personal FM System, in which students with mild hearing loss wear a receiver and headphones.

162

		• Teachers should help parents recognize and take advantage of the many opportunities for auditory training and learning around the house. • Speechreading was traditionally called *lipreading*, but understanding speech from visual clues involves more than simply looking at the lips. • Speechreading skills of deaf students can be improved by practicing lipreading their own speech and that of others via computer-assisted video instruction (DeFilippo, Sims, & Gottermeier, 1995; Sims & Gottermeier, 1995). • Another technological development that promises to increase access by deaf persons during live presentations, such as public or classroom lectures, is known as *real-time translation*. A trained operator listens to the lecture and types a shorthand code into a laptop computer, and special software produces an instantaneous display of the transcription that can be projected on a screen. After the presentation, the student can obtain a printout of the transcript.	• Gallaudet also has programs to train teachers of deaf children. Both deaf and hearing students are accepted into these programs.
Teaching & Learning in School: Tips for Facilitating Communication	• Keeping your whole face visible, speaking directly to the deaf person, and using visual aides are among several tips provided to facilitate communication through speechreading, sign language, or written communication, three common ways that deaf persons communicate.	
Educational Services Alternatives	• Thirty-five percent of children with hearing loss attend regular classrooms, 20% attend resource rooms for part of the school day, 30% are served in separate classrooms, and 10% go to residential schools. • All of the professional and parent organizations involved in deaf education have issued position statements strongly in favor of maintaining a continuum of placement options.	

163

	• The *Rowley* case was the first Supreme Court case to be argued by a lawyer who is deaf. • Many leaders in the Deaf community are strong advocates against the development and use of technology designed to "cure" deafness, particularly the use of cochlear implants with deaf children.
Profiles & Perspectives: I Am Not Disabled—I'm Just Deaf	• A Deaf young man gives his views of being deaf, the use of American Sign Language, and inclusion. One of the main reasons that mainstreaming is not good is because mainstreaming lacks Deaf Culture and ASL.
Current Issues and Future Trends	• Given the large percentage of children with hearing loss who are educated in regular classrooms for most of the day, it is likely that oral/aural and total communication methods of instruction will continue to be used. • The bilingual-bicultural approach will probably be used with a growing percentage of the deaf children served in special schools and self-contained classrooms. • Although technology holds much promise for addressing the communication problems faced by deaf and hard of hearing people, many leaders of the deaf culture do not view deafness as a disability and oppose efforts to "cure" it or make them more like the mainstream hearing culture. • Access to the language and communication modality best suited to their individual needs and preferences, effective instruction with meaningful curriculum, and self-advocacy are the keys to improving the future for people who are deaf or hard of hearing.

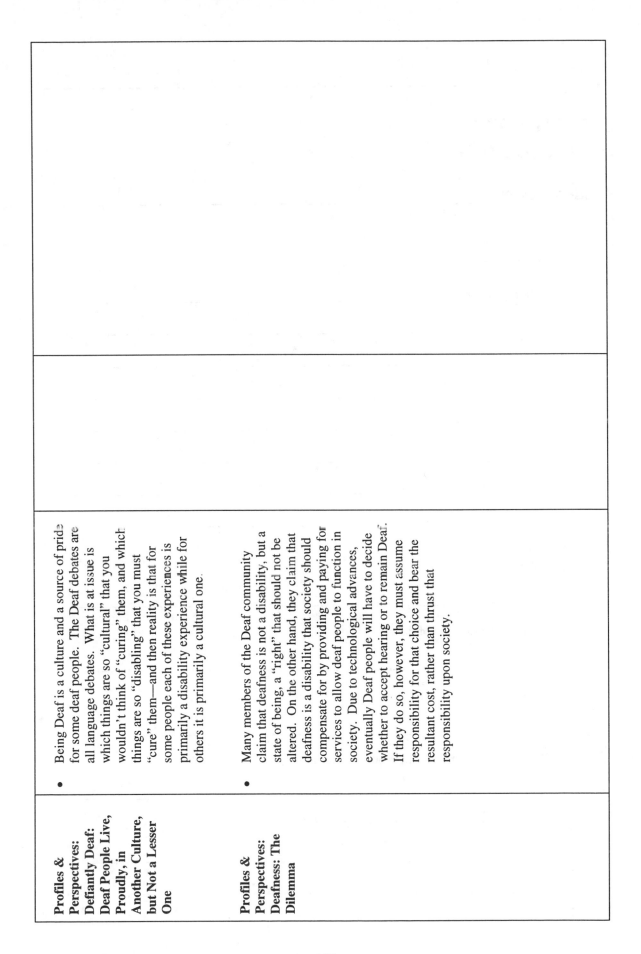

Profiles & Perspectives: Defiantly Deaf: Deaf People Live, Proudly, in Another Culture, but Not a Lesser One

- Being Deaf is a culture and a source of pride for some deaf people. The Deaf debates are all language debates. What is at issue is which things are so "cultural" that you wouldn't think of "curing" them, and which things are so "disabling" that you must "cure" them—and then reality is that for some people each of these experiences is primarily a disability experience while for others it is primarily a cultural one.

Profiles & Perspectives: Deafness: The Dilemma

- Many members of the Deaf community claim that deafness is not a disability, but a state of being, a "right" that should not be altered. On the other hand, they claim that deafness is a disability that society should compensate for by providing and paying for services to allow deaf people to function in society. Due to technological advances, eventually Deaf people will have to decide whether to accept hearing or to remain Deaf. If they do so, however, they must assume responsibility for that choice and bear the resultant cost, rather than thrust that responsibility upon society.

165

CHAPTER TEN
HEARING LOSS

Guided Review

I. Defining Hearing Loss
    A. What are the definitions of the following terms?

        1. hearing impairment: _____

            _____

        2. deaf: _____

            _____

        3. residual hearing: _____

            _____

        4. hard of hearing: _____

            _____

    B. How We Hear
        1. What is audition?

            a) _____

        2. What is the function of the ear?

            a) _____

        3. How does the auricle function?

            a) _____

        4. How does the tympanic membrane (eardrum) work?

            a) _____

        5. What happens to sound as it enters the middle ear?

            a) _____

                _____

6. What are the organs of the inner ear and how do they function?

a) _____

b) _____

C. The Nature of Sound
   1. How is sound measured?

   a) _____

   b) _____

II. Prevalence
   A. How many people have a chronic hearing loss?

   1. _____ out of every 1,000 people

   2. _____ million Americans experience some difficulty receiving and processing aural communication.

   3. _____ percent of individuals over age 75

   B. How many students received special education services under the disability category of hearing impairments in the 1996-97 school year?

   1. _____ students ages 6 to 21

   2. _____ percent of all school-age children receiving special education

   3. _____ percent of the resident student population

III. Types and Causes of Hearing Loss
   A. What are the two main types of hearing loss and how are they caused?

   1. _____

   2. _____

   B. Define the following terms.

   1. mixed hearing loss: _____

   2. unilateral: _____

   3. bilateral: _____

   4. congenital: _____

   5. adventitious: _____

6. prelingual: _____

7. postlingual: _____

   C. What are the prelingual causes of hearing loss?

     1. _____

     2. _____

     3. _____

     4. _____

   D. What are the postlingual causes of hearing loss?

     1. _____

     2. _____

     3. _____

IV. Identification and Assessment
   A. What is pure-tone audiometry?

     1. _____

     2. _____

   B. What is speech audiometry?

     1. _____

   C. What are the types of alternative audiometric techniques?

     1. _____

     2. _____

     3. _____

     4. _____

     5. _____

   D. What are the degrees of hearing loss?

     1. _____

     2. _____

     3. _____

4. _____

5. _____

V. Effects of Hearing Loss
   A. English Literacy and Academic Achievement
     1. What are the effects of hearing loss on acquiring English language skills?

       a) _____

       b) _____

       c) _____

     2. What are the effects of hearing loss on academic achievement?

       a) _____

       b) _____

   B. Social and Psychological Factors
     1. How does impaired hearing influence a child's socioemotional development?

       a) _____

       b) _____

       c) _____

VI. Educational Approaches
   A. Oral/Aural Approaches
     1. What methods are used in an oral/aural program?

       a) _____

       b) _____

     2. What is cued speech?

       a) _____

   B. Total Communication
     1. What does the total communication approach advocate?

       a) _____

     2. What types of manual communication are used in the total communication approach?

       a) _____

       b) _____

C. Bilingual-Bicultural Approach
    1. How do proponents of the bilingual-bicultural model view deafness?

        a) _____

    2. What is American Sign Language?

        a) _____

        b) _____

        c) _____

D. Controversy and Choices
    1. How should educators determine which approach is appropriate?

        a) _____

VII. Assistive Listening Devices and Other Support Technologies
  A. Amplification Instruments
    1. What are the benefits and limitations of hearing aids?

        a) _____

        b) _____

    2. How are hearing aids most effectively used?

        a) _____

        b) _____

        c) _____

  B. Auditory Training
    1. What are the levels of auditory training?

        a) _____

        b) _____

        c) _____

        d) _____

  C. Speechreading
    1. What are the limitations of speechreading?

        a) _____

        b) _____

        c) _____

        d) _____

D. What is an interpreter?

    1. _____

E. What is a text telephone?

    1. _____

F. What is television captioning?

    1. _____

G. How are alerting devices used?

    1. _____

VIII. Educational Service Alternatives

A. What are the most important ingredients for the deaf or hard of hearing child's success in the regular classroom (Davis, 1986)?

    1. _____

    2. _____

    3. _____

    4. _____

    5. _____

B. What is the most fundamental factor for determining success?

    1. _____

C. What does the research say about where deaf children are most appropriately taught?

    1. _____

    2. What is the position of professional and parent organizations involved with educating deaf students?

        a) _____

D. Postsecondary Education

    1. What are some institutions that offer special programs to students with hearing loss?

        a) _____

        b) _____

c) _____

d) _____

e) _____

f) _____

2. What percentage of students with hearing loss go on to receive higher education?

a) _____

IX. What Are the Current Issues and Future Trends of Educating Students with Hearing Loss?

A. _____

B. _____

C. _____

D. _____

CHAPTER TEN
HEARING LOSS

Objectives

1. Define *deaf* and *hard of hearing*.

2. Explain how hearing loss is measured.

3. Identify the prevalence of students with hearing loss.

4. Explain how prelingual and postlingual hearing loss influences language development.

5. Describe the causes of prelingual and postlingual hearing loss.

6. Explain how children with hearing loss are identified.

7. Explain how hearing loss influences educational performance.

8. Describe the following educational approaches: oral/aural approach, total communication, and bilingual-bicultural approach.

9. Describe the various types of assistive listening devices and support technologies for people with hearing loss.

10. Describe the educational placement alternatives for children with hearing loss.

Self-check Quiz

1. By what age can hearing children discriminate the speech sounds of the language to which they have been exposed from the sounds of other languages?
    a. 1 year
    b. 3 months
    c. 6 months
    d. 2 years

2. Under what conditions can children who are deaf acquire language and communication skills in a manner quite similar to the acquisition of speech by hearing children?
    a. when they are exposed to a visual, sign-based language as their first language
    b. when they are exposed to oral/aural communication
    c. when they receive a cochlear implant
    d. when they are sent to a residential school at a young age

3. The average deaf child might accurately speechread about _____ of what is said.
   a. 5%
   b. 25%
   c. 10%
   d. 20%

4. Why is a person who is hard of hearing more like a normally hearing person than a deaf person?
   a. both use vision as the primary mode for speech and language development
   b. both use audition as the primary mode for speech and language
   c. both use vision and audition equally as the mode for speech and language
   d. none of the above

5. What is the main receptor organ for hearing?
   a. eardrum
   b. ossicles
   c. auricle
   d. cochlea

6. Elena's hearing loss is 70 decibels. This means that Elena has a hearing loss that affects her ability to:
   a. hear very low frequency sounds.
   b. hear very high frequency sounds.
   c. understand talking at normal conversational volumes.
   d. all of the above

7. What population has the largest percentage of individuals with a hearing loss?
   a. individuals over age 75
   b. individuals under age 5
   c. individuals between age 6 and 21
   d. individuals between age 22 and 74

8. Lindsey's hearing loss occurred when she was born. Which of the following statements is accurate?
   a. Lindsey's hearing loss is postlingual and as a result will require an emphasis on acquisition of language and communication.
   b. Lindsey's hearing loss is prelingual and as a result will require an emphasis on communication.
   c. Lindsey's hearing loss is postlingual and as a result will require an emphasis on maintenance of intelligible speech and appropriate language patterns.
   d. Lindsey's hearing loss is prelingual and as a result will require an emphasis on maintenance of intelligible speech and appropriate language patterns.

9. Shakera is a 5-year-old with an adventitious hearing loss. This means that:
   a. Shakera was born with a hearing loss.
   b. Shakera has a unilateral hearing loss.
   c. Shakera's hearing loss was acquired after birth.
   d. none of the above

10. Camille pushes a lever in the presence of a light paired with sound. When she does this, she is reinforced by the test examiner with a token. The audiometric technique used to test Camille is called:
    a. pure-tone audiometry.
    b. impedance audiometry.
    c. behavior observation audiometry.
    d. operant conditioning audiometry.

11. What is the average reading level of 18-year-old deaf or hard of hearing students?
    a. 1st–2nd
    b. 3rd–4th
    c. 5th–6th
    d. 7th–8th

12. According to Schirmer, when is the appropriate time for a teacher to focus a student's attention on syntax within the writing process?
    a. during the editing stage
    b. during the first written draft
    c. during the conference stage where the student selects a topic and audience
    d. throughout the whole writing process from start to finish.

13. Which of the following is the most fundamental factor in determining how successful a student with hearing impairments will be in a regular classroom or any other placement?
    a. average or above-average intelligence
    b. adequate support services, such as speech therapy
    c. quality of instruction
    d. oral communication skills

14. Which of the following describes the predominant method of instruction in schools for the deaf?
    a. fingerspelling and signing
    b. signing and speech
    c. oral language
    d. American Sign Language

15. Which of the following is NOT an accurate statement about American Sign Language (ASL)?
    a. ASL is the language of the Deaf culture in the United States and Canada.
    b. ASL has its own vocabulary, syntax, and grammatical rules which correspond to spoken or written English.
    c. ASL is seldom used within a total communication program.
    d. Space and movement play important linguistic roles in ASL.

CHAPTER ELEVEN
BLINDNESS AND LOW VISION

Focus Questions

- **In what ways does loss of vision affect learning?**

Consider all the events in the environment that are perceived through vision. Hearing, taste, touch, and smell help to add detail to what is seen, but it is vision that plays the critical role in learning to interact with the various features of the environment. Sighted individuals may take for granted all of the information obtained through the eyes and the relative ease with which this visual information is learned. It is not difficult to make a list of the academic skills that children with visual impairment will have difficulty learning because of the absence or distortion of visual information. But learning is not limited to academics. Knowing when a classmate or teacher is disappointed or pleased, eating without embarrassment in the school cafeteria, and interaction appropriately in social situations are also largely dependent on visual information. Special instructional methods and equipment are often necessary for children with visual impairment to help them acquire the academic and social skills necessary for independent and productive living.

- **How does the age at which vision is lost affect the student?**

One factor that influences instructional decisions for children with visual impairment is the point in the child's life when the vision loss occurred. Congenital visual impairment are present at birth. Adventitious visual impairment are acquired at some point during a person's life. A child who is adventitiously blind usually retains some visual memory, and the teacher can take advantage of the images the child recalls when designing teaching programs and instructional activities. Teaching the words "dog" and "blue" will be much easier if the child has seen a dog or things that are blue. Children with a congenital visual impairment, however, have no visual history and will often require educational programming that makes use of their nonvisual experiences. Learning what dogs are can be accomplished through the sense of touch, but touching dogs is not the same as seeing dogs. Concepts such as blueness, as simple as they are for most normally sighted children to learn, may be impossible for children with a congenital visual impairment to understand. Additionally, the level of emotional support and acceptance will differ for children who are adventitiously blind and congenitally blind. The child who must make a sudden adjustment to the loss of vision will probably require a great deal of emotional support.

- **Normally sighted children enter school with a great deal of knowledge about trees. How could a teacher help the young child who is congenitally blind learn about trees?**

In developing an answer to this question, you must first eliminate any temptation to use visual information. Because the visual impairment has been present since birth, the child has a total absence of visual memory. Verbal descriptions of the tree may add something to the child's understanding, but the teaching approach will have to rely primarily on direct, firsthand contact with trees through child's other senses. This design of the teaching program must allow the child to experience a wide range of tactile, olfactory, auditory, and other sensory stimuli, all of which add to the essence of a tree and help convey that trees are of different sizes, shapes, and types. This teaching approach for the concept of a tree will be similar to the teaching approach for the many other concepts that students with visual impairment must learn.

- **What compensatory skills do students with visual impairment need?**

  A basic goal of special education concerns teaching skills for independent and productive living. Academic skills alone will not accomplish this goal. Learning life skills such as cooking, grooming, managing money, participating in leisure activities, and coping with societal expectations are essential parts of any curriculum for exceptional learners. In addition, children with visual impairment should know how to explain their disability to others and to refrain from behaviors such as rocking and head rolling that draw undue and often negative attention to their disabilities. Because most students with visual impairment are educated in regular school settings, it is easy to focus attention exclusively on academic skills. It is important to recognize, however, that academics are but one part of a curriculum necessary to prepare students with visual impairment for life beyond the classroom.

- **How do the educational goals and instructional methods for children with low vision differ from those for children who are blind?**

  As do children in all other categories of exceptionality, children with visual impairment exhibit a wide range of abilities. Children, who are identified as blind, generally have little or no useful vision. Children with low vision, on the other hand, often have residual vision so that with various types of ocular aids, such as large print or magnifiers, they can use printed materials in their classrooms and communities. The challenge to special education teachers is to tailor instruction to the needs and abilities of each individual. Children with visual impairment have different levels of visual ability, but the goal of instruction is the same for all these children: to teach them skills that will enable them to take their place in society as productive, self-sufficient individuals.

Chapter Overview

Legal definitions of blindness are based on a person's ability to see clearly at specified distances (visual acuity) and the restrictiveness in a persons' peripheral vision. Educational definitions focus on the effects of these impairment on the child's learning. Children with visual impairment display a wide range of visual capacities, from blindness—the total absence of useful vision—to low vision—which can be quite useful for learning. All of these students, however, require special educational modifications to assist their progress in regular educational programs.

The age of onset of a visual impairment is an important consideration in programming. Children who have been blind from birth have no visual history to apply to their current learning needs. Adventitiously blind children, on the other hand, have had some visual experiences, which typically facilitate the teaching of many skills.

The prevalence of visual impairment is low. Approximately 1 in 1,000 children of school age have visual impairment. About one-third of all students with visual impairment have additional disabilities. In spite of this low prevalence, visual impairment have historically been an educational priority, and services are provided by a large network of advocacy groups. Some understanding of the medical reasons for the visual impairment may be helpful to the teacher, but an understanding of the educational implication is much more important.

Children with visual impairment can fully participate in the programs a school has to offer. By using Braille and a host of manipulative, technological, and optical aids, children with visual impairment can participate in academic programs with their normally sighted peers. Academics cannot, however, be the exclusive focus of educational programs. Gaining social skills, meeting expectations, finding suitable work, exploring sexuality, and other basic life experiences are as important as academics. In addition, specialized training in orientation and mobility is essential to ensuring the independence of students who are blind or have low vision.

CHAPTER ELEVEN AT A GLANCE

MAIN TOPICS	KEY POINTS	KEY TERMS	MARGIN NOTES
Defining Visual Impairment	• Legal blindness is defined as visual acuity of 20/200 or less in the better eye after correction with glasses or contacts, or a restricted field of vision of 20% or less. • An educational definition considers the extent to which a visual impairment makes special education materials or methods necessary. • Children with low vision can learn through the visual channel, and many learn to read print. • Besides impairments in visual acuity and field of vision, a child may have problems with ocular motility or visual accommodation, photophobia, or defective color vision. • The age at onset of a visual impairment affects a child's educational and emotional needs.	• visual acuity • Snellen chart • legally blind • field of vision • peripheral vision • totally blind • functionally blind • braille • low vision	• Some people, with or without correction, have visual acuity that is better than 20/20. If the vision in one of your eyes is rated as 20/10, for example, you can see from 20 feet what the "20/20" eye must be within 10 feet to see.
Prevalence	• A visual impairment is a low-incidence disability, affecting approximately 5 of every 10,000 children in the school-age population. About one-third of all students with visual impairments have additional disabilities.		

Types and Causes of Visual Impairment	• The eye collects light reflected from objects, focuses the objects' image on the retina, and transmits the image to the brain. Difficulty with any part of this process can cause vision problems. Common types of visual impairment include:
	  • Myopia (nearsightedness)
	  • Hyperopia (farsightedness)
	  • Astigmatism (blurred vision caused by irregularity in the cornea or other surfaces)
	  • Cataract (blurred or distorted vision caused by cloudiness in the lens)
	  • Glaucoma (loss of vision caused by high pressure within the eye)
	  • Diabetic retinopathy, retinitis pigmentosa, macular degeneration, and retinal detachment (all caused by problems with the retina)
	  • Retinopathy of prematurity (retrolental fibroplasia) (caused by administration and withdrawal of high doses of oxygen to premature infants in incubators)
		• retina
		• cornea
		• aqueous humor
		• pupil
		• iris
		• lens
		• vitreous humor
		• refractive errors
		• optometrist
		• ophthalmologist
		• myopia
		• hyperopia
		• astigmatism
		• ocular motility
		• binocular vision
		• strabismus
		• amblyopia
		• accommodation
		• nystagmus
		• cataract
		• glaucoma
			• An **optometrist** specializes in the evaluation and optical correction of refractive errors. An **ophthalmologist** is a physician who specializes in the diagnosis and treatment of eye diseases and conditions.

Educational Approaches	• Teachers of children with visual impairments need specialized skills, along with knowledge, competence, and creativity. • Most children who are blind learn to read braille and write with a brailler and a slate and stylus. They may also learn to type and use special equipment for mathematics, social studies, and listening to or feeling regular print.	• optical character recognition (OCR) • contractions • brailler • visual efficiency • stereotypic behavior • orientation • mobility • O&M specialists • peripatologists	• Bender (1994) describes how individuals who are blind can learn to identify birds in the field by developing their listening skills. • Although the cost of some assistive technology, such as the Optacon or Kurzweil Personal Reader, is prohibitive for many people, low-interest loans and financial assistance can sometimes be arranged (Uslan, 1992).

	• sighted guide technique	• McComisky (1996) describes a braille readiness grid designed to help early childhood special educators identify skills and activities that will foster enthusiasm for reading and learning braille in preschoolers with visual impairments. Pester (1993) makes recommendations for braille instruction for individuals who are blind adventitiously. • Teachers determine the most appropriate reading medium for students with visual impairments by conducting the Learning Media Assessment (Koenig & Holbrook, 1993). • Barraga's *Program to Develop Efficiency in Visual Functioning* is available from the American Printing House for the Blind. • Children whose vision is extremely limited are more likely to use monocular (one-eye) than binocular (two-eye) aids, especially for seeing things at a distance. • Some students with low vision who read print are also taught to read braille, especially if their visual acuity is expected to decrease because of a degenerative eye condition (Holbrook & Koenig, 1992). • Gellhaus and Olson (1993) offer numerous suggestions for using color and contrast to improve the educational environment of students with visual impairments with multiple disabilities. • Recorded books and magazines and the equipment to use them can be obtained through the Library of Congress, the American Printing House for the Blind, Recordings for the Blind, the Canadian National Institute for the Blind, and various other organizations, usually on a free-loan basis. Each state has a designated library that provides books and materials for blind readers.
Teaching & Learning in School: Helping the Student with Low Vision	• Children with low vision should learn to use their residual vision as efficiently as possible. Many use optical aids and large print to read regular type. • All children with visual impairments need to develop their listening skills. • Most students with visual impairments also need special instruction in practical daily living skills, interpersonal skills, and human sexuality. • Some children with visual impairments need help in reducing or eliminating stereotypic behaviors. • The teacher must use direct observation and a variety of informal and formal procedures to assess children with visual impairments. Standardized intelligence tests are often inappropriate. • Orientation and mobility (O&M) instruction is a must for individuals who are blind or have severe visual impairments.	• Teachers of students with low vision should: verbalize as much as possible; give the student the original from which the ditto is made; pay attention to the contrast, print style, and spacing; encourage the child to accept the responsibility of seeking help when necessary; shorten or allow more time for assignments that involve copying; and allow the child to hold printed material close to the eyes.

	• Don't be afraid to use words such as "look" and "see" when talking with a person who is blind. Individuals with visual impairments use these words too.
	• Pava (1994) conducted a national survey of 161 women and men with visual impairments to assess their perceived vulnerability to sexual and physical assault. Although women respondents perceived themselves to be more at risk for assault than men, one in three of all the respondents reported having been targets of attempted or actual assault at some point in their lives.
	• In some states, O&M specialists are called *peripatologists*.
	• Although the long cane is a relatively simple and sturdy piece of equipment, it takes a beating during training and everyday use. In anticipation of "the inevitable need to repair canes," O&M specialist Tom Langham (1993) always carries a tool kit that includes such items as pliers, hacksaw, pipe cutter, Allen wrenches, red and white reflective tape, wax, and a bent coat hanger.
	• Clarke (1988) describes a large number of mobility devices for preschoolers with visual impairments and multiple disabilities. She also provides a checklist by which parents, teachers, and O&M specialists can compare and evaluate the relative advantages and disadvantages of the different devices.
	• Sighted people must realize that guide dogs are not pets, but working companions for their owners (Ulrey, 1994). Don't pet a guide dog without first seeking the owner's permission. Do not take hold of the dog's harness as this might confuse the dog and the owner.
Teaching & Learning in School: I Made It Myself, and It's Good!	• Young adults who were blind were taught to use tape-recorded recipes played on a small audiocassette recorder to cook from recipes. Pre-recorded audio prompts can be individualized for each student, can provide self-delivered prompts in a private, unobtrusive and normalized manner that does not impose on or bother others, and can allow control over the environment.

181

		• The June 1993 issue of the *Journal of Visual Impairment and Blindness* is devoted to residential schools.
	• itinerant teacher-consultants • vision specialist	
Educational Service Alternatives	• Most children with visual impairments spend at least part of each school day in regular classes with sighted peers. • In many districts, a specially trained itinerant vision specialist provides support for students with visual impairments and their regular classroom teachers. • Some programs also have separate orientation and mobility instructors or separate resource rooms for students with visual impairments. • About 12% of the children with visual impairments, especially those with other disabilities, attend residential schools. • Most parents can choose between public day and residential schools for their children with visual impairments.	
Teaching & Learning in School: Including Ryan: Using Natural Supports to Make Inclusion Natural	• Adults in the classroom provided supports to Ryan through contextual cues, spontaneous events, detailed verbal directions and explanations, simple verbal cues and prompts, and physical cues. Peers were another viable and natural source of information about and assistance in the environment. Ryan also used a variety of adaptive strategies that enabled him to move freely within the classroom environment and gain access to information.	

Current Issues and Future Trends	• Children with visual impairments are likely to receive specialized services in the future in both regular and residential schools. Greater emphasis will be placed on intervention with visually impaired infants and young children and on training older students for independence.
	• It is hoped that all people with visual impairments will benefit from new technological and biomedical developments. Artificial sight may be possible in the future.
	• Career opportunities will likely expand, as individuals with visual impairments become more aware of their legal and human rights.

CHAPTER ELEVEN
BLINDNESS AND LOW VISION

Guided Review

I. Defining Visual Impairment
    A. What is the legal definition of visual impairment based upon?

        1. _____

        2. _____

    B. Educational Definitions of Visual Impairments
        1. What is the definition of a visual impairment according to IDEA?

            a) _____

                _____

        2. What are the educational definitions of the following terms?

            a) totally blind: _____

            b) functionally blind: _____

            c) low vision: _____

    C. How does the age of onset of visual impairments affect learning?

        1. _____

        2. _____

II. Prevalence
    A. What is the prevalence of children with visual impairments?

        1. _____ children in 10,000

        2. _____ children between ages 6 to 21

        3. _____ percent of the entire school-age population

III. Types and Causes of Visual Impairment
    A. Through which parts of the eye do light rays pass?

        1. _____

2. _____

3. _____

4. _____

5. _____

B. Refractive Errors
   1. Define the following types of refractive errors:

   a) myopia _____

       _____

   b) hyperopia: _____

       _____

   c) astigmatism: _____

       _____

   d) ocular motility: _____

       _____

   e) strabismus: _____

       _____

   f) amblyopia: _____

       _____

   g) nystagmus: _____

       _____

   h) cataract: _____

       _____

   i) glaucoma: _____

       _____

IV. Educational Approaches
   A. Special Adaptations for Students Who Are Blind
      1. What are examples of tactile aids and manipulatives?

      a) _____

      b) _____

185

c) _____

d) _____

e) _____

f) _____

2. What are examples of technological aids used for reading print?

    a) _____

    b) _____

3. What categories of assistive technology are available to people with visual impairments?

    a) _____

    b) _____

4. The Braille System
    a) What devices are used for Braille writing?

       1) _____

       2) _____

5. What recent technological aids have made Braille more efficient?

    a) _____

    b) _____

6. What did the 1997 amendments to IDEA specify in response to the concern over declining Braille literacy?

    a) _____

    _____

B. Special Adaptations for Students with Low Vision
    1. What basic premises about low vision should guide instructional planning?

       a) _____

       _____

       b) _____

       _____

       c) _____

d) _____

e) _____

f) _____

_____

g) _____

h) _____

_____

2. Visual Functioning
   a) What four goals should instructional activities be based upon (Corn, 1989)?

   1) _____

   2) _____

   3) _____

   4) _____

3. What kinds of optical devices can children with low vision use?

   a) _____

   b) _____

   c) _____

   d) _____

   e) _____

4. What three basic approaches are used for reading print?

   a) _____

   b) _____

   c) _____

   d) What other variables besides print size should be considered when using printed materials with students with low vision?

   1) _____

   2) _____

3) _____

4) _____

5. What other classroom modifications can be made for students with low vision?

    a) _____

    b) _____

    c) _____

    d) _____

C. Listening
  1. Listening involves what types of skills?

    a) _____

    b) _____

    c) _____

    d) _____

  2. How may good listening skills help a student with a visual impairment?

    a) _____

    _____

D. Daily Living and Social Skills
  1. What do reviews of the literature on social skills of children with visual impairments indicate?

    a) _____

  2. What is one explanation for why students with visual impairments engage in less social _ interaction?

    a) _____

  3. How can stereotypic behavior place students at a disadvantage?

    a) _____

E. Why is human sexuality an issue for children with visual impairments?

  1. _____

  _____

F. Why is there concern about the use of IQ tests with visually impaired students?

    1. _____

G. Define *orientation* and *mobility.*

    1. Orientation: _____

    2. Mobility: _____

    3. How is the long cane used for traveling?

        a) _____

    4. What are the limitations of the long cane?

        a) _____

    5. How are guide dogs used?

        a) _____

    6. What are the guidelines for being a sighted guide?

        a) _____

        b) _____

        c) _____

        d) _____

        e) _____

V. Educational Service Alternatives
  A. Public Schools
    1. What are the responsibilities of most itinerant teacher-consultants?

        a) _____

        b) _____

        c) _____

        d) _____

        e) _____

        f) _____

        g) _____

        h) _____

B. Residential Schools
   1. What advantages were specified for attending residential schools (Livingston et al., 1985)?

   a) _____

   b) _____

   c) _____

   d) _____

   e) _____

VI. Current Issues and Future Trends
   A. Which schools will likely serve children with visual impairment in the future?

   1. _____

   B. What future technological advances may be available for people with visual impairment?

   1. _____

   2. _____

   C. Fighting Against Discrimination
      1. What will the future bring regarding employment opportunities for people with visual impairment?

      a) _____

         _____

         _____

CHAPTER ELEVEN
BLINDNESS AND LOW VISION

Objectives

1. Explain the differences between the legal and educational definitions of visual impairment.

2. Discuss how the age of onset of visual impairment influences a student's educational and emotional needs.

3. Identify the prevalence of visual impairment.

4. List and describe the types and causes of visual impairment.

5. Discuss how the educational approaches differ for children who are blind and children who have low vision.

6. Discuss the importance of teaching listening skills to children who are blind or have low vision.

7. Define *orientation* and *mobility*, and discuss the importance of orientation and mobility instruction.

8. Explain the various educational service alternatives for children who are blind or have low vision.

9. Describe the emerging technological advances designed to help people who are blind or have low vision.

Self-check Quiz

1. The legal definition of visual impairment is based on:
   a. visual acuity and field of vision.
   b. visual acuity and the extent to which the person learns through the visual channel.
   c. the extent to which the person learns through other senses.
   d. depth perception and peripheral vision.

2. A child who learns primarily through the hearing and tactile channels, but may also use limited vision to supplement the information received from auditory and tactile senses:
   a. is totally blind.
   b. is functionally blind.
   c. has low vision.
   d. is legally blind.

3. Which refractive error refers to distorted or blurred vision caused by irregularities in the cornea or other surfaces of the eye?
   a. myopia
   b. hyperopia
   c. strabismus
   d. astigmatism

4. A child who is congenitally blind:
   a. retains a visual memory of things they formerly saw.
   b. may need greater emotional support because of the sudden adjustment to the loss of vision.
   c. has a background of learning primarily through hearing and touch.
   d. all of the above

5. Students with visual impairment make up what percentage of the entire school-age population?
   a. less than 0.1%
   b. more than 2.5%
   c. approximately 1.0%
   d. approximately 0.5%

6. _____ is a prevalent disease marked by abnormally high pressure within the eye caused by disturbances or blockages of fluids.
   a. Cataracts
   b. Astigmatism
   c. Glaucoma
   d. Nystagmus

7. Which of the following technological aids reads printed text via a synthetic voice?
   a. Speech-Plus talking calculator
   b. Kurzweil Personal Reader
   c. VersaBraille II+
   d. Optacon

8. How has IDEA (1997) addressed the concern over declining Braille literacy?
   a. For students with visual impairment, IEP teams must make a determination of the student's preferred reading medium, and instruction in Braille must be considered.
   b. IEP teams must plan for reading instruction in Braille for all students with severe visual impairment.
   c. Before attempting Braille instruction, IEP teams must first develop objectives for reading adapted print materials.
   d. IDEA has not addressed the concern over declining Braille literacy.

9. Curriculum development and instructional planning should be guided by which of the following premises?
   a. Clinical measurements should dictate visual functioning.
   b. Those with low vision can enhance visual functioning through the use of optical aids, nonoptical aids, environmental modifications, and/or techniques.
   c. Those with low vision will not be able to develop a sense of visual beauty.
   d. all of the above

10. Visual efficiency includes which of the following skills?
    a. controlling eye movements
    b. paying attention to visual stimuli
    c. processing visual information rapidly
    d. all of the above

11. Which of the following is NOT a basic approach for reading print materials?
    a. approach magnification
    b. lenses
    c. large print
    d. learning to read Braille

12. Which of the following is NOT a factor to consider when using printed materials to teach children with low vision?
    a. quality of the material
    b. spacing between the lines
    c. illumination of the setting in which the child reads
    d. noise level of the setting in which the child reads

13. Which of the following statements is true?
    a. IQ tests are standardized on both sighted children and children with visual impairment.
    b. IQ tests give an accurate picture of the abilities and needs of students with visual impairment.
    c. Many children with visual impairment have been placed in inappropriate educational programs because of reliance on standardized test performance.
    d. none of the above

14. What is the most widely used device for adults with severe visual impairment who travel independently?
    a. guide dogs
    b. laser beam cane
    c. long cane
    d. electronic travel aids

15. Which of the following is NOT a recommended part of the sighted guide technique?
    a. The sighted guide should speak in a normal tone of voice and ask directly, "May I help you?"
    b. The person with visual impairment should lightly grasp the sighted person's arm just above the elbow and walk half a step behind the sighted person.
    c. The sighted guide should walk at a slower pace than normal.
    d. The sighted guide should place the hand of the person with visual impairment on the back of the chair.

CHAPTER TWELVE
PHYSICAL IMPAIRMENTS AND SPECIAL HEALTH CARE NEEDS

Focus Questions

- **In what ways might the visibility of a physical or health impairment affect a child's self-perception, social development, and level of independence across different environments?**

Earlier in the text the relative nature of disabilities was discussed—a disability might lead to educational, personal, or social problems in one setting, while in another setting not be handicapping at all. Although this is true for all disabilities, it may be more obvious for the child with a physical or health disability. For example, a child with an artificial limb may be handicapped when competing against nondisabled peers on the baseball field, but experience no handicap in the classroom. Also, students with physical disabilities will have different learning experiences in different environments depending upon how individuals in those environments act towards them. For example, students with physical disabilities are likely to have markedly different and perhaps more challenging outdoor experiences in a camp setting where counselors are comfortable working with them than in a camp setting where counselors are overly concerned about their physical or health disabilities.

- **How do the nature and severity of a child's physical disability affect IEP goals and objectives?**

When a child with physical disabilities needs special education, an IEP is developed. Students with physical disabilities may require modifications in the physical environment, teaching techniques, or other aspects of their educational programs. Some children with physical disabilities are extremely restricted in their activities, whereas others have few limitations on what they can do or learn. The goals and objectives of the IEP must match the individual needs of the child with physical disabilities. Modifications in the learning environment, including both physical and instructional adaptations, must be reflected in the IEP.

- **What are some of the problems that members of an interdisciplinary team for a child with severe physical disabilities and multiple health needs must guard against?**

No other group of exceptional children comes into contact, both in and out of school, with as many different teachers, physicians, therapists, and other specialists. Because the medical, educational, therapeutic, vocational, and social needs of students with physical and health impairments are often complex and frequently affect each other, it is especially important that educational and health care personnel openly communicate and cooperate with one another.

- **How might an assistive technology device be a hindrance as well as a help?**

Special devices or adaptations often are necessary for children with physical or health impairments to function successfully. There is, however, an unfortunate side effect to them: their use makes the disability more conspicuous. The more conspicuous the disability, the more inclined others might be to react to the disability first and to the child as a person second. All children need to develop positive views of themselves, and inappropriate reactions from parents, teachers, classmates, and others have a decidedly negative impact on a child's self-esteem.

- **Of the many ways in which the classroom environment and instruction can be modified to support the inclusion of students with physical and health impairments, which are most important?**

Teachers of children with physical and health impairments frequently find it necessary to adapt equipment, schedules, or settings so that their students can participate more fully in educational and recreational activities. Although there is currently an increasing trend toward integrating children with physical and health problems, this practice has raised several controversial issues. These issues revolve around determining the extent to which teachers and schools should realistically be expected to care for students with physical and health-related disabilities. Decisions concerning the safety for all students must be made. Those activities in which the child with the physical disability can be socially accepted and contribute to the group must be included in the educational program.

Chapter Overview

When you first thought about becoming a teacher, how did you envision your job? What did you think would be your primary teaching responsibilities? You probably envisioned teaching days similar to those of your elementary teachers. Most teachers' responsibilities include activities such as teaching academic lessons, giving tests, taking attendance, planning field trips, filling out report cards, and dealing with occasional behavior problems. If you thought much about becoming a teacher of exceptional children, you probably thought your experiences would be a bit different. Teachers of exceptional children often teach different content, use alternative instructional activities, and, depending on the type of exceptionality, deal with more classroom behavior problems. But did you ever think that as a teacher you might be expected to adjust braces or prosthetic devices on a child, care for a child having a seizure or in diabetic shock, or provide intermittent catheterization (removing urine from a child who does not have effective bladder control)? Probably not.

Yet, recent developments in assistive technology, biomedical engineering, and medical treatment are making it possible for more and more children who need these types of services to be educated in schools. Approximately 3.8% of school-age children who receive special education services were reported under the disability categories of orthopedic impairment, other health impairments, and traumatic brain injury. About one third of these students are served in regular classrooms. Fortunately, with accurate and up-to-date information about how to deal effectively with various physical and health conditions, more teachers are becoming confident and skilled in creating effective yet safe educational settings for these students.

This chapter provides information about the nature and effects of various physical impairments. It is important for those who work with these students to understand how a particular condition might affect a child's learning, development, and behavior. Some children with cerebral palsy show only mild symptoms and need few modifications or adaptations. Others may have little or no control over their arms, legs, or speech, and may also have impaired vision or hearing. Children with osteogenesis imperfecta, an inherited condition marked by bones that are extremely brittle, are literally fragile and must be protected. Children who have suffered serious injuries to the head often experience temporary or lasting symptoms, including cognitive and language deficits, memory loss, seizures, and perceptual disorders. In addition, these children often display inappropriate or exaggerated behaviors, ranging from extreme aggressiveness to apathy. The chapter also presents information about the characteristics and education of children with chronic illnesses and other health-related conditions. Although chronic illnesses are generally less visible than orthopedic and neurological impairments, their effects on a child may be just as great.

The last half of the chapter reviews several other issues related to physical and health-related impairments, including: (a) the prevalence of different physical and health impairments, (b) the historical background of education for these children, (c) educational implications and interventions, (d) educational service alternatives, and (e) current issues and future trends.

CHAPTER TWELVE AT A GLANCE

MAIN TOPICS	KEY POINTS	KEY TERMS	MARGIN NOTES
Types of Physical Impairments and Special Health Needs	• Children with physical and health impairments are a widely varied population and include children eligible for special education under three disability categories of IDEA: orthopedic impairments, other health impairments, and traumatic brain injury. • Orthopedic impairments involve the skeletal system; a neurological impairment involves the nervous system; they are frequently described in terms of the affected parts of the body. • Cerebral palsy is a long-term condition arising from impairment to the brain and causing disturbances in voluntary motor functions. • Spina bifida is a congenital condition that may cause loss of sensation and severe muscle weakness in the lower part of the body. Children with spina bifida can usually participate in most classroom activities but need assistance in toileting. • Muscular dystrophy is a long-term condition; most children gradually lose the ability to walk independently. • Spinal cord injuries are caused by a penetrating injury, stretching of the vertebral column, fracture of the vertebrae, or compression of the spinal cord and usually result in some form of paralysis below the site of the injury.	• orthopedic impairment • neurological impairment • plegia • monoplegia • hemiplegia • triplegia • quadriplegia • paraplegia • diplegia • double hemiplegia • cerebral palsy • prenatal • perinatal • postnatal • hypertonia • hypotonia • generalized hypotonia • athetosis • ataxia • rigidity • tremor • spina bifida • spina bifida occulta • meningocele • myelomeningocele • neural tube defect • hydrocephalus • shunt	• Some children with attention deficit/hyperactivity disorder (ADHD) who meet eligibility requirements for special education are served under the other health impairments category of IDEA; others are served under the specific learning disability or serious emotional disturbance categories. • The children most frequently served in special education programs for orthopedic impairments are those with cerebral palsy. In some programs, half or more of the students considered to have physical or health impairments have cerebral palsy. • Because most children with cerebral palsy have diffuse brain damage, "pure" types of cerebral palsy are rare (Jones, 1983). • The motor impairment of children with cerebral palsy often makes it frustrating, if not impossible, for them to play with toys. • The term *neural tube defect* is sometimes used to describe spina bifida and similar impairments. • Most of the approximately 7,000 to 10,000 persons in the United States who are victims of traumatic spinal cord injuries each year are 15 to 25 years old (Laskowski-Jones, 1993). • Proper positioning and regular movement are critical for students who use wheelchairs.

Other Health Impairments include: • Seizure disorders (epilepsy) that produce disturbances of movement, sensation, behavior, and/or consciousness. • Diabetes is a disorder of metabolism that can often be controlled with injections of insulin. • Children with cystic fibrosis, asthma, hemophilia, HIV/AIDS, or other chronic health conditions may require special education and other related services, such as health care services and counseling. • Traumatic brain injury is a significant cause of neurological impairments and learning problems.	• catheter • clean intermittent catheterization (CIC) • muscular dystrophy • Duchenne muscular dystrophy (DMD) • limb deficiency • prosthesis • seizure • seizure disorder • epilepsy • generalized tonic-clonic seizure • absence seizure • complex partial seizure • simple partial seizure • diabetes mellitus • diabetic retinopathy • hypoglycemia • hyperglycemia • asthma • cystic fibrosis • hemophilia • acquired immunodeficiency syndrome (AIDS) • human immunodeficiency virus (HIV)	• Many unfortunate misconceptions about epilepsy have circulated in the past and are still prevalent even today. Negative public attitudes, in fact, have probably been more harmful to people with epilepsy than has the condition itself. • *Diabetic retinopathy* is a leading cause of blindness in adults. • Estimates of the number of school days lost each year because of asthma range from 10 million (Majer & Joy, 1993) and 130 million if hay fever is included (McLaughlin & Nall, 1994). • Getting children with cystic fibrosis to consume enough calories is critical to their health and development. Stark et al. (1993) used a behaviorally based treatment intervention that included nutrition education, rewards for meeting gradually increasing calorie goals, and relaxation training to successfully increase calorie consumption and growth rates of three children with cystic fibrosis. Increased calorie consumption was maintained at a two-year follow-up. • Students receiving special education services may be more prone to contracting HIV because of lack of knowledge about the disease. • When it was originally passed, IDEA did not specifically mention the needs of children who have experienced head trauma and/or coma; however, when the law was amended in 1990 (P.L. 101-476), traumatic brain injury was added as a new disability category under which children could be eligible for special education services.

		• Each year about 65,000 children and adults are treated in hospital emergency rooms for head injuries as a result of bicycle accidents. Most of those injuries would be avoided if riders wore safety helmets (Raskin, 1990).
		• *Chronic* conditions are present over long periods and tend not to get better or disappear. An *acute* condition, in contrast, is severe but of limited duration. • Many people with disabilities report that their hardware creates a great deal of curiosity and leads to frequent, repetitive questions from strangers. Learning how to explain their physical disabilities or health condition and to respond to questions can be an appropriate component of the educational programs for some children. They may also benefit from discussing concerns such as when to ask for help from others and when to decline offers of assistance.
		• chronic condition • acute condition
Prevalence	• In 1995–96, 3.8% of all school-age students who received special education services were reported under the disability categories of orthopedic impairments, other health impairments, and traumatic brain injury. • This figure does not include all children who have physical or health impairments because some are reported under other disability categories.	
Variables Affecting the Impact of Physical Impairments and Chronic Health Conditions		• Perrin et al. (1993) have proposed a noncategorical system for classifying and understanding children's chronic physical and medical conditions; it includes 13 dimensions that are judged on a continuum from mild to profound. • Many factors must be taken into consideration when assessing the effects of a physical impairment or health condition on a child's development and behavior. Three particularly important variables are the age of onset, the severity with which the condition affects different areas of functioning, and the visibility of the impairment.

	• physical therapists (PTs) • occupational therapists (OTs) • Individualized Health Care Plan (IHCP or IHP) • assistive technology	• Incidentally, a student should not be described as being "confined to a wheelchair." This expression suggests that the person is restrained or even imprisoned. Actually, most students who use wheelchairs leave them from time to time to exercise or to lie down. It is preferable to say that a student "has a wheelchair" or "uses a wheelchair to get around." A working knowledge of techniques associated with wheelchair use can be helpful to a teacher in reducing problems and making classrooms and school buildings accessible (Venn, Morgenstern, & Dykes, 1979). • Students who are able to use their arms should be taught to perform "chair pushups" in which they lift their buttocks off the seat for 5 to 10 seconds. Doing chair pushups every 30 to 60 minutes may prevent pressure sores. Children who cannot perform pushups can shift their weight by bending forward and sideways (Hoeman, 1996). • Handi-Hams is an international organization of people with and without disabilities who help people with physical disabilities expand their world through amateur radio. • Often, well-meaning teachers, classmates, and parents tend to do too much for a child with a physical or health impairment. It may be difficult, frustrating, and/or time-consuming for the child to learn to care for his own needs, but the confidence and skills gained from independent functioning are well worth the effort in the long run. • Children should be taught to *never* equate a person with a disability label, as in "He's a C.P." or "She's an epileptic."
Educational Approaches	• Children with physical and health impairments typically require services from an interdisciplinary team of professionals. • Physical therapists (PTs) use specialized knowledge to plan and oversee a child's program in making correct and useful movements. Occupational therapists (OTs) are concerned with a child's participation in activities, especially those that will be useful in self-help, employment, recreation, communication, and other aspects of daily living. • Students with physical and health impairments can increase their independence by learning to take care of their personal health-care routines such as clean intermittent catheterization and self-administration of medication. • Adaptations to the physical environment and to classroom activities can enable students with physical and health impairments to participate more fully in the school program. • Proper positioning and seating is important for children with physical disabilities. A standard routine for lifting and moving a child with physical disabilities should be followed by all teachers and other staff. • Assistive technology is any piece of equipment or device used to increase, maintain, or improve functional capabilities of individuals with disabilities. • How parents, teachers, classmates, and others react to a child with physical disabilities is at least as important as the disability itself.	

Teaching & Learning in School: Using Dolls to Teach Self-catheterization Skills to Children with Spina Bifida	• Successful reentry of children who have missed extended periods of school because of illness or the contraction of a disease requires preparation of the child, his or her parents, classmates, and school personnel. • When complex procedures must be performed by children or persons with learning problems, direct systematic instruction is indicated. If the procedures involve invading the body or errors during practice are potentially hazardous, simulation training can be used.
Teaching & Learning in School: Adapting Toys for Children with Cerebral Palsy	• Stabilization, boundaries, grasping aids, manipulation aids, and switches are modifications most effective in promoting active, independent use of play materials.
Educational Service Alternatives	• About one third of students with physical impairments and chronic health conditions are served in regular classrooms. • The amount of supportive help that may be required to enable a student with physical disabilities to function effectively in a regular class varies greatly, according to each child's condition, needs, and level of functioning. • Special classes usually provide smaller class size, more adapted equipment, and easier access to the services of professionals such as physicians, physical and occupational therapists, and specialists in communication disorders and therapeutic recreation.
medically fragile	• The term *medically fragile* is sometimes used to refer to students who are dependent on life-support medical technology. As Lehr and McDaid (1993) point out, however, many of these children are "incredibly strong—survivors of many adverse conditions, who in fact are not fragile at all, but remarkably strong to be able to rebound from periods of acute illness" (p. 7). They believe the term *medically fragile* frightens school personnel and should not be used.

Current Issues and Future Trends		
		• Reed Martin, an attorney who specializes in special education law, recommends that teachers who perform health care procedures for students have liability insurance (*CEC Today*, 1998). • Telethons and other fund-raising activities on behalf of persons with disabilities have become controversial in recent years. Some self-advocacy groups and professionals believe they perpetuate negative stereotypes and portray people with disabilities as objects of pity (see the November 1993 issue of the *TASH Newsletter*).
	• myoelectric (bionic) limbs • robotics	
Current Issues and Future Trends **Profiles & Perspectives: Grasping the Future with Robotic Aids**	• Some technology dependent children require home- or hospital-based instruction because their life-support equipment cannot be made portable. • The education of students with physical and health impairments in regular classrooms has raised several controversial issues, especially with regard to the provision of medically related procedures and services in the classroom. • New and emerging technologies such as bionic body parts and robot assistants offer exciting possibilities for the future. • Animals, particularly dogs and monkeys, can assist people with physical disabilities in various ways. • Children with physical disabilities can gain self-knowledge and self-confidence by meeting capable adults with disabilities and joining self-advocacy groups. • Using robotics to increase the manipulation potential of persons with severe physical disabilities is an area that is receiving growing attention from rehabilitation engineers and technologists in the schools.	

CHAPTER TWELVE
PHYSICAL IMPAIRMENTS AND SPECIAL HEALTH CARE NEEDS

Guided Review _____

I. Types of Physical Impairments and Special Health Care Needs
   A. Orthopedic and Neurological Impairments
      1. What are terms used to describe the body parts affected by orthopedic and neurological impairments?

         a) _____

         b) _____

         c) _____

         d) _____

         e) _____

         f) _____

         g) _____

      2. Cerebral Palsy
         a) What are the types of cerebral palsy?

            1) _____

            2) _____

            3) _____

            4) _____

      3. Spina Bifida
         a) What are the three types of spina bifida?

            1) _____

            2) _____

            3) _____

    b)   What is hydrocephalus?

        1)   _____

4.   What is muscular dystrophy?

    a)   _____

5.   Spinal Cord Injuries
    a)   What are the causes of most spinal cord injuries?

        1)   _____

        2)   _____

        3)   _____

    b)   What are the usual effects of spinal cord injuries?

        1)   _____

        2)   _____

6.   Limb Deficiency
    a)   What are the causes of limb deficiencies?

        1)   _____

        2)   _____

B.   Other Health Impairments
   1.   Seizure disorders
      a)   What are the types of seizures?

        1)   _____

        2)   _____

        3)   _____

        4)   _____

C.   Juvenile Diabetes
   1.   What are the symptoms of hypoglycemia and hyperglycemia?

      a)   hypoglycemia: _____

              _____

      b)   hyperglycemia: _____

              _____

D. What is asthma?

1. _____

_____ _____

E. What is cystic fibrosis?

1. _____

_____

F. What is hemophilia?

1. _____

G. What is Acquired Immune Deficiency Syndrome?

1. _____

2. What are the implications and recommendations concerning AIDS?

a) _____

b) _____

c) _____

d) _____

H. Traumatic Brain Injury (TBI)
1. What modifications can assist children with TBI during the reentry period?

a) _____

b) _____

c) _____

d) _____

e) _____

f) _____

II. Prevalence
A. How many children with physical and health impairments were served during the 1996-97 school year?

1. _____ with orthopedic impairments

2. _____ with health impairments

3. _____ with TBI

III. What are the variables affecting the impact of physical impairments and chronic health conditions?

A. _____

B. _____

C. _____

IV. Educational Approaches
A. Which professionals are included in the interdisciplinary team?

1. _____

2. _____

3. _____

4. _____

5. _____

6. _____

7. _____

8. _____

B. Environmental Modifications
1. What are some adaptations which can be made to the physical environment?

a) _____

b) _____

c) _____

d) _____

e) _____

f) _____

g) _____

C. Special Health Care Needs
1. What are some specialized procedures necessary for some students with physical and health care needs?

a) _____

b) _____

c) _____

d) _____

e) _____

2. Importance of Positioning, Seating, and Movement
   a) What adjustments can contribute to improved appearance, greater comfort, and increased health for children with physical disabilities?

   1) _____

   2) _____

   3) _____

   4) _____

3. Lifting and Transporting Students
   a) Routines for lifting, transferring, and repositioning children should entail standard procedures for:

   1) _____

   2) _____

   3) _____

   4) _____

D. Assistive Technology
   1. How should mobility devices be selected?

   a) _____

   b) _____

   c) _____

   d) _____

   e) _____

E. Inclusive Attitudes
   1. How can teachers effectively accept and treat children with physical disabilities?

   a) _____

   b) _____

   c) _____

   d) _____

V. Educational Service Alternatives
   A. Where are students with physical disabilities served?

      1. _____

      2. _____

      3. _____

VI. What Are the Current Issues and Future Trends for Educating Children with Physical and Health Impairments?

   A. _____

   B. _____

   C. _____

   D. _____

CHAPTER TWELVE
PHYSICAL IMPAIRMENTS AND SPECIAL HEALTH CARE NEEDS

Objectives

1. Define *orthopedic* and *neurological impairments*.

2. Describe the following physical disabilities or health impairments: cerebral palsy, spina bifida, muscular dystrophy, spinal cord injuries, seizure disorders, diabetes, cystic fibrosis, asthma, hemophilia, HIV/AIDS, and traumatic brain injury.

3. Identify the prevalence of children with physical and health impairments.

4. Describe the educational implications for students with physical and health impairments.

5. Explain the job of the physical therapist and the occupational therapist.

6. Describe how the physical environment of the classroom can be adapted to accommodate children with physical disabilities.

7. Describe and give examples of how assistive technology can improve the functional capabilities of individuals with disabilities.

8. Explain the various types of educational service alternatives for children with physical disabilities or health impairments.

9. Describe the new and emerging technologies that can help individuals with physical disabilities.

Self-check Quiz

1. Which of the following physical/health impairments involves a lesion to the brain and creates disturbances of voluntary motor functions?
   a. muscular dystrophy
   b. cerebral palsy
   c. spina bifida
   d. epilepsy

2. The term for a congenital defect in the formation of the spinal cord and the overlying bones of the vertebrae is:
   a. meningocele.
   b. muscular dystrophy.
   c. spina bifida.
   d. myelomeningocele.

3. The most common form of a group of long-term diseases that progressively weaken and waste away the body's muscles is:
   a. Duchenne muscular dystrophy.
   b. osteogenesis imperfecta.
   c. arthritis.
   d. cystic fibrosis.

4. Mr. and Mrs. Grace are the parents of a preschooler with cerebral palsy. They know the importance of play for their child and are concerned that he has trouble playing with many of the toys he has. What adaptations could be suggested to these parents for making their son's toys more accessible to him?
   a. clamping toys with a base to a table
   b. placing push toys on a tray with edges to create a restricted area
   c. placing pull toys on a track
   d. all of the above

5. When PL 94-142 was amended in 1990, which of the following disability categories was added?
   a. limb deficiency disabilities
   b. muscular dystrophy
   c. traumatic brain injury
   d. epilepsy

6. Insulin shock can occur as a result of:
   a. not taking enough insulin.
   b. taking too much insulin.
   c. missing or delaying a meal.
   d. both b & c

7. Leslie, a student in second grade, frequently drops his pencil and stares blankly into space for several seconds. Leslie is usually a well-behaved, attentive student, so his teacher is at a loss to explain his periodic inattention. Which of the following seizures would explain Leslie's inattention?
   a. complex partial seizures
   b. generalized tonic-clonic seizures
   c. grand mal seizures
   d. absence seizures

8. Which of the following is true for Davida, an infant who has the HIV virus?
   a. Davida, like any child with AIDS, can legally be excluded from public school.
   b. Davida will develop AIDS; all persons who have the HIV virus develop AIDS.
   c. Davida may have significant neurological complications and developmental delays.
   d. Davida must have gotten the virus from a transfusion of infected blood since that is the only way an infant can get the virus.

9. Children most frequently placed in special education programs for physical, orthopedic, or health impairments are those with:
   a. muscular dystrophy.
   b. cerebral palsy.
   c. spina bifida.
   d. cystic fibrosis.

10. Bernadette is a 10-year-old student who has been unable to attend public school because of her health impairment. What educational services is her local school district obligated to provide for her?
    a. The school district is not obligated to provide educational services for any student whose physical condition does not allow him/her to attend school.
    b. If Bernadette's medical condition necessitates hospitalization or treatment at home for 90 days or more, the school district is obligated to provide an itinerant teacher for her.
    c. If Bernadette's condition necessitates hospitalization or treatment at home for 30 days or more, t he school district is obligated to draw up an IEP and provide appropriate educational services to Bernadette through a qualified teacher.
    d. The school district is obligated to provide educational opportunities that allow Bernadette to interact with nondisabled students.

11. Phoebe has cerebral palsy. One arm and one leg are affected. Which of the following terms is MOST descriptive of Phoebe's condition?
    a. diplegic
    b. hemiplegic
    c. quadriplegic
    d. triplegic

12. Which of the following teachers is NOT using cautionary behaviors for Donald, who has diabetes?
    a. Mrs. Morton lets Donald use fifteen minutes of his lunch hour to complete his math assignment.
    b. Mr. Nestor keeps candy bars in her desk.
    c. Mr. Sabatino encourages Donald to participate in physical education activities but watches closely the strenuous nature of the activity.
    d. none of the above

13. Which of the following poses a serious threat to individuals with hemophilia?
    a. minor cuts and scrapes
    b. most physical activity
    c. internal bleeding
    d. all of the above

14. To a child with physical disabilities, what is as important as the disability itself?
    a. how parents, teachers, classmates, and others react to the child's disability
    b. mental ability to function within the regular class
    c. to communicate needs orally
    d. mobility to move within an educational setting

15. If there are students in your class with physical or health impairments, what will be your role regarding these students' ambulation devices?
    a. daily observing the students' use and care of their equipment
    b. designing a barrier-free classroom
    c. encouraging maximum use of ambulation devices in the classroom, the school, the home, and the community
    d. all of the above

CHAPTER THIRTEEN
SEVERE DISABILITIES

Focus Questions

• **Why is a curriculum based on typical developmental stages inappropriate for students with severe disabilities?**

Developmental theories of learning assume that children pass through an orderly sequence of developmental stages. These stages are the basis for determining what kinds of skills are appropriate for instruction and when those skills should be taught. For example, if a child has not yet developed the physical dexterity necessary to properly hold a pencil, teaching the child to write will usually not begin until the child is developmentally "ready." A curriculum based on typical developmental stages, however, is unlikely to meet the needs of students with severe disabilities. For children with severe disabilities, learning such basic skills as getting from place to place independently, communicating, controlling bowel and bladder functions, and self-feeding cannot wait for a readiness stage to be reached. Instruction in these skills, all of which influence the individual's quality of life, must begin when individuals with severe disabilities need to learn them, not when they are developmentally ready to learn them. The "everyday skills" that normally developing children learn almost effortlessly present substantial challenges for individuals with severe disabilities.

• **For what reasons is it especially critical to select functional, age-appropriate curriculum objectives for students with severe disabilities?**

Educational programs for students with severe disabilities are future oriented in their efforts to teach skills that will enable students with severe disabilities to participate in integrated settings as meaningfully and independently as possible after they leave school.

• **How can the principle of partial participation contribute to the quality of life for a student with severe disabilities?**

Most of us feel good when we are able to do things for ourselves. In addition, most of us think highly of others who can accomplish things independently. For individuals with severe disabilities, complete independence may be impossible with many tasks. Partial participation provides an opportunity for the person with the disability to perform the steps of a task that he or she can do, and it also provides an opportunity for the person and the caregiver to interact in a natural manner that is mutually beneficial. Independence is fostered, learned helplessness is discouraged, and both individuals have performed important work worthy of praise.

• **What are the benefits for students with severe disabilities who are educated in regular, integrated schools? What are potential disadvantages?**

The benefits of being educated in a regular school setting are the same for students with severe disabilities as they are for any other student. Consider the different opportunities and experiences available to students who have equal and, to the maximum extent possible, unlimited access to educational programs in normalized, mainstream settings. Next, consider the inherent limitations that exist when a student's access to these opportunities is restricted or absent. The benefits of being educated in integrated schools is especially critical for students with severe disabilities because the school may be the only environment in which they are guaranteed access to the learning opportunities that will promote increased independence. In general, integrated schools provide opportunities to participate in meaningful activities, provide parents and families greater access to school activities, and provide an opportunity for exceptional learners to develop social relationships with their nondisabled peers. The potential disadvantage is that the functional IEP goals and objectives for students with severe disabilities are seldom reflected in the academic curriculum of the regular classroom (especially at secondary level).

- **What benefits might students who are not disabled experience from the inclusion of peers with severe disabilities in the regular classroom?**

  Nondisabled students who go to school with their disabled peers are more likely to be tolerant and supportive of and to develop relationships with individuals who are considered "different" by society at large. Accepting differences in other people is a skill that must be learned in much the same manner as learning reading or math. Learning to accept individuals with disabilities without the opportunity to interact with them would be like learning to add without being exposed to numbers. Although the majority of students with severe disabilities are still educated in segregated settings, this practice is steadily changing as the benefits of more inclusive settings to both disabled and nondisabled students continue to be demonstrated.

Chapter Overview

Individuals with severe disabilities have begun to enjoy the benefits of an educational system that has shifted from custodial caretaking to educational programming. Today a philosophy of inclusion promotes the integration of individuals with severe disabilities into the mainstream of society. This trend is significantly different from the philosophy that promoted institutionalization from infancy.

It is well documented that students with severe disabilities can learn, do learn, and with appropriate teaching and support, lead productive lives. Individuals with severe disabilities usually learn even the most basic everyday skills very slowly. However, each person with severe disabilities is a unique individual complete with a diverse set of strengths and weaknesses. One goal of special education for individuals with severe disabilities is to teach them to take full advantage of their strengths as a means of compensating for their weaknesses.

No universally accepted definition of severe disabilities exists, and this lack of a precise definition makes prevalence estimates difficult. Although no single set of behaviors is common to all individuals with severe disabilities, this population is often characterized by severe deficits in communication skills, physical and motor development, self-help skills and by excesses of maladaptive or inappropriate behavior. Students with severe disabilities, of course, also have many positive attributes and display warmth, humor, and sociability.

The causes of severe disabilities are often traced to biological influences that result in brain damage. Chromosomal abnormalities, genetic disorders, complications during pregnancy or the birthing process, as well as head trauma and disease later in life can all cause severe disabilities. The specific cause of many severely disabling conditions, however, is not known.

Educational programming for students with severe disabilities has changed dramatically from the not-so-distant past when automatic institutionalization and little or no instruction or training were the norm. Today, least restrictive educational placements are mandated, and the trend is toward educating students with severe disabilities in regular school settings. Such placements generally provide educational and social benefits not only for students with disabilities but for their nondisabled peers as well. The educational curriculum focuses primarily on functional skills, choice-making skills, and recreation/ leisure skills that will enable students with severe disabilities to experience success in the present and prepare them to be as independent as possible in the future. Unlike their nondisabled peers, most students with severe disabilities do not learn through imitation or other indirect means; they require well planned, highly structured, and precisely delivered, and carefully evaluated instruction.

Methods of managing incidents of inappropriate, maladaptive, and aggressive behavior have also undergone philosophical and procedural changes. The use of restraints and other methods that would not be considered acceptable with nondisabled individuals are generally being replaced with procedures that respect the individual student and are aimed at preparation for independent living in normalized settings. Good teaching does more than eliminate or reduce inappropriate behaviors. Good teaching focuses on setting the occasion for new behaviors that are appropriate and useful to the student to be acquired, maintained, and generalized.

Individuals with severe disabilities present many challenges to the field of special education, but these challenges should not be viewed as burdens. Most of us do our best work when faced with challenges that demand our best. Educating students with severe disabilities is a dynamic, changing area of special education and one that influences the direction of the field as a whole. The opportunity to work with individuals with severe disabilities can provide tremendous personal and professional rewards.

CHAPTER THIRTEEN AT A GLANCE

MAIN TOPICS	KEY POINTS	KEY TERMS	MARGIN NOTES
Defining Severe Disabilities	• The student with severe disabilities needs instruction in many of the basic skills that most children without disabilities acquire without instruction in the first 5 years of life. • Students with profound disabilities have pervasive delays in all domains of functioning at a developmental level no higher than 2 years. • TASH defines persons with severe disabilities as "individuals of all ages who require extensive ongoing support in more than one major life activity in order to participate in integrated community settings and to enjoy a quality of life that is available to citizens with fewer or no disabilities."	• severe disabilities • profound disabilities	• An extended school year is used to meet the requirements of a free, appropriate public education for some students with severe disabilities. • *Journal of the Association for Persons with Severe Disabilities* (JASH) is a primary source for the latest research and conceptual developments in educating learners who are challenged by severe disabilities.
Profiles & Perspectives: Are All Children Educable?	• Children, no matter how severe their disabilities, have the right to the best possible public education and training society can offer them. Students with the most severe disabilities will go no farther than people let them; it is up to us to open doors and to raise our sights, not to create additional barriers.		
Characteristics of Students with Severe Disabilities	• Students with severe disabilities frequently have multiple disabilities, including physical problems, and usually look and act markedly different from children without disabilities.	• deaf-blindness • autism • savant syndrome	• The intellectual level of students with dual sensory impairments ranges from giftedness (as in the case of Helen Keller) to profound mental retardation.

- It is difficult to assess accurately the degree of sensory impairments in most students with deaf-blindness because additional disabilities or other barriers to communication limit the students' responses to typical testing procedures (Wolf, Delk, & Schein, 1982).

- Curricula for assessing and teaching functional communication skills to students who are deaf-blind have been developed by the Perkins School (1978) and the Alabama Institute for the Deaf-Blind (1989).

- Some clinicians use the term *pervasive developmental disorder* to describe the developmental and behavioral characteristics of autism.

- Although the precise cause of autism is unknown, recent research suggests a biological or organic origin (Mauk, Reber, & Batshaw, 1997; Rutter & Schopler, 1987).

- Not all children with autism exhibit sensory deficit characteristics. Many can be "quite loving and caring, thoughtful and creative" (Greenspan & Weider, 1997, p. 88).

- Facilitated communication is a controversial method of assisting persons with autism and other nonverbal individuals to communicate.

- The cognitive ability of about 80% of individuals with autism is similar to that of persons with mental retardation (Ritvo & Freeman, 1978). A very few persons with autism exhibit **savant syndrome**, an extraordinary ability in an area such as memorization, mathematics, or music while functioning at the mental retardation level in all other areas (Treffert, 1989).

- Children with severe disabilities frequently show some or all of the following behaviors or skill deficits: slow acquisition rates for learning new skills, difficulty in generalizing and maintaining newly learned skills, severe deficits in communication skills, impaired physical and motor development, deficits in self-help skills, infrequent constructive behavior and interaction, and frequent inappropriate behavior.

- Despite their intense challenges, students with severe disabilities often exhibit many positive characteristics, such as warmth, sociability, and persistence.

- Students with dual sensory impairments cannot be accommodated in special education programs designed solely for students with hearing or visual impairments. Although the vast majority of children labeled deaf-blind have some functional hearing and/or vision, the dual impairments severely impede learning of communication and social skills.

- The essential features of autism typically appear prior to 30 months of age and consist of disturbances of (a) developmental rates and/or sequences; (b) responses to sensory stimuli; (c) speech, language, and cognitive capacities; and (d) capacities to relate to people, events, and objects.

• Only 12% of school-age children with autism were served in regular classrooms and special schools during the 1995–1996 school year (U.S. Department of Education, 1998).	
Profiles & Perspectives: The Autism Wars • Although the prognosis for children with autism has traditionally been poor, some children have achieved normal functioning by the primary grades as a result of an intensive, behaviorally oriented program of early intervention and preschool mainstreaming. • Despite their limitations, children with severe disabilities can and do learn. • "The Autism Wars" refers to the fierce infighting and conflicting claims of individuals or groups, each of whom claims to know how best to treat children with autism, and each of whom derides the theories and methods of the other camps. The barrage of conflicting messages can produce a sense of frustration, fear and even despair for those new to the field of autism.	
Prevalence • Students with severe and multiple disabilities are served and counted under several disability categories, making prevalence figures hard to determine. • Estimates of the prevalence of severe disabilities range from 0.1% to 1% of the population.	

	• Coulter (1994) states that a brain disorder is "the only condition that will account for the existence of profound disabilities" (p. 41). • Severe disabilities can be caused by most of the organic causes of mental retardation.	• Gothelf, Crimmins, Mercer, and Finocchiaro (1994) describe a 10-step method for teaching choice making to students who are deaf-blind. • Rowland and Schweigert (1993) have developed an environmental inventory that enables teachers to analyze specific activities that encourage functional communication. Reichle and Keogh (1986) discuss decision-making rules for selecting the most appropriate methods of communication for students with severe disabilities.
		• facilitated communication (FC) • partial participation • positive behavioral support • functional assessment
Causes of Severe Disabilities	• Brain disorders, which are involved in most cases of severe intellectual disabilities, are the result of either brain dysgenesis (abnormal brain development) or brain damage (caused by influences that alter the structure or function of a brain that had been developing normally up to that point). • Severe and profound disabilities most often have biological causes, including chromosomal abnormalities, genetic and metabolic disorders, complications of pregnancy and prenatal care, birth trauma, and later brain damage. • In about one sixth of all cases of severe disabilities, the cause cannot be clearly determined.	• A curriculum based on typical developmental milestones is inappropriate for most students with severe disabilities. • Students with severe disabilities must be taught skills that are functional, age-appropriate, and directed toward the community. Interaction with nondisabled students should occur regularly. • Students with severe disabilities should be taught choice-making skills. • The emphasis of research and training in communication for persons with severe disabilities has shifted from the remediation of specific forms of communication to a focus on functional communication of any mode that enables communication partners to establish shared meanings.
Educational Approaches		

217

- Effective instruction requires structure and precision. Skills must be broken down into small steps; current performance must be precisely assessed; the target skill must be stated clearly; and skills must be taught in an appropriate sequence.

- Some students with severe disabilities use augmentative and alternative systems of communication (AAC), such as gestures, various sign language systems, pictorial communication boards, symbol systems, and electronic communication aids.

- Facilitated communication (FC) is a process by which a communication partner, called a facilitator, provides physical support to assist an individual who cannot speak or whose speech is limited to typing on a keyboard or to pointing at pictures, words, or other symbols on a communication board.

- Although proponents claim that FC enables some people with autism and moderate or severe mental retardation to display an "undisclosed literacy" consistent with "normal intellectual functioning," scientific research to date has not confirmed those claims.

- Students with severe disabilities should also be taught age-appropriate recreation and leisure skills.

- Because each student with severe disabilities has many learning needs, teachers must carefully prioritize and choose IEP objectives and learning activities that will be of most benefit to the student and his or her family.

- Advocates of FC contend that objective evaluation of FC is not important because the benefits are potentially large and the procedure carries little risk (e.g., Haskew & Donnellan, 1992). Unfortunately, use of FC has not been without risks; there have been criminal investigations of parents, family members, or other caretakers falsely accused of maltreatment or abuse via FC-produced communication (Johnson, 1994).

- Family involvement in the identification and prioritization of IEP skills and objectives, of course, is not only important for students with severe disabilities. This strategy can also be used in the development of all IEPs.

- Choral responding and response cards enable every student in the group to respond to each instructional trial.

- Increased social contacts and positive social acceptance with peers without disabilities as a result of inclusion have been reported by a number of other researchers as well (e.g., Evans, Salisbury, Palombaro, Berryman, & Hollowood, 1992; Hunt, Farron-Davis, Beckstead, Curtis, & Goetz, 1994; Romer & Haring, 1994).

- Billinglsey and Kelley (1994) reported that 39 of 51 instructional methods considered to be "best practice" for educating students with severe disabilities are considered acceptable and appropriate for use in general education classrooms.

Effective instruction of students with severe disabilities is characterized by these elements:

- The student's current level of performance must be precisely assessed.
- The skill to be taught must be defined clearly.
- The skills must be ordered in an appropriate sequence.
- The teacher must provide a clear prompt or cue to the student.
- The students must receive immediate feedback and reinforcement from the teacher.
- Strategies that promote generalization of learning must be used.
- The student's performance must be carefully measured and evaluated.

- Partial participation is both a philosophy for selecting activities and a method for adapting activities and supports to enable students with severe disabilities to actively participate in meaningful tasks they are not able to perform independently.

- The teacher of students with severe disabilities must be skilled in positive, instructionally relevant strategies for assessing and dealing with challenging and problem behaviors.

- Research and practice are providing increasing support for the use of integrated group instruction arrangements with students with severe disabilities.

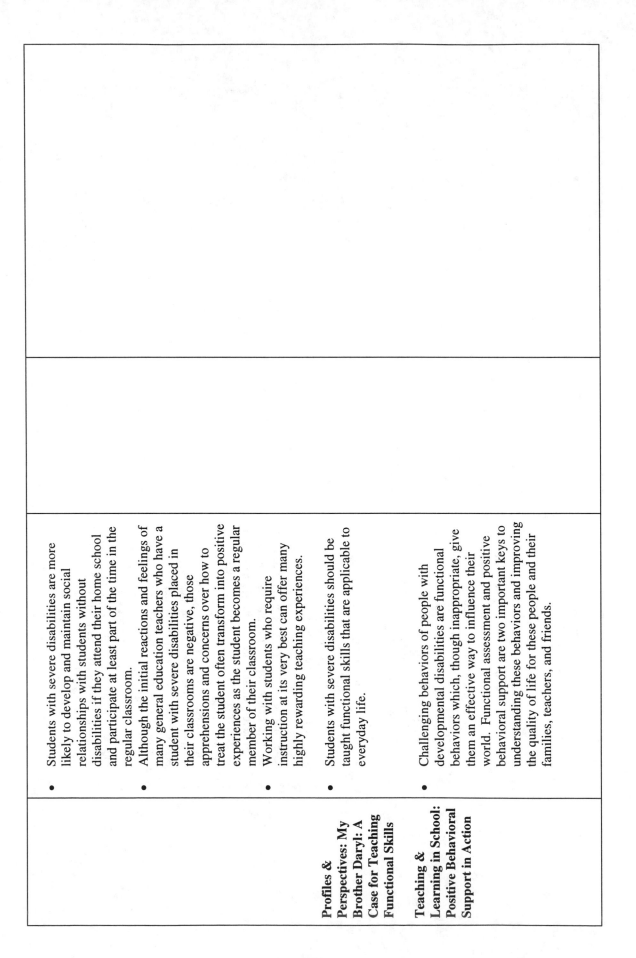

- Students with severe disabilities are more likely to develop and maintain social relationships with students without disabilities if they attend their home school and participate at least part of the time in the regular classroom.

- Although the initial reactions and feelings of many general education teachers who have a student with severe disabilities placed in their classrooms are negative, those apprehensions and concerns over how to treat the student often transform into positive experiences as the student becomes a regular member of their classroom.

- Working with students who require instruction at its very best can offer many highly rewarding teaching experiences.

- Students with severe disabilities should be taught functional skills that are applicable to everyday life.

- Challenging behaviors of people with developmental disabilities are functional behaviors which, though inappropriate, give them an effective way to influence their world. Functional assessment and positive behavioral support are two important keys to understanding these behaviors and improving the quality of life for these people and their families, teachers, and friends.

Profiles & Perspectives: My Brother Daryl: A Case for Teaching Functional Skills

Teaching & Learning in School: Positive Behavioral Support in Action

Teaching & Learning in School: Planning for Inclusion with MAPS

- MAPS, the McGill Action Planning System, is a systems approach to problem solving that has helped many schools welcome and support children with disabilities in regular schools and classrooms.

Teaching & Learning in School: The Metropolitan Nashville Peer Buddy Program

- The Metropolitan Nashville Peer Buddy Program attempts to remove scheduling barriers to inclusion by providing daily class times in which general education and special education students may interact. Buddies serve as positive role models for social interaction and provide the support their partners need to be included within general education and vocational classes and the extracurricular activities that make up a typical high school day.

CHAPTER THIRTEEN
SEVERE DISABILITIES

Guided Review

I. Defining Severe Disabilities
   A. Most educators now maintain that developmental levels have little relevance to this population and instead emphasize that a student with severe disabilities is one who needs:

      1. _____

      2. _____

      3. _____

      4. _____

   B. According to IDEA, children with severe disabilities are children who need:

      1. _____

      2. _____

   C. According to Sternberg (1994), an individual with profound disabilities exhibits profound developmental disabilities in what five behavior-content areas?

      1. _____

      2. _____

      3. _____

      4. _____

      5. _____

II. Characteristics of Students with Severe Disabilities
   A. What behaviors are frequently observed in students with severe disabilities?

      1. _____

      2. _____

      3. _____

      4. _____

5. _____

6. _____

7. _____

B. Deaf-Blindness
   1. How does IDEA define *deaf-blindness*?

      a) _____

   2. What do education programs for students with deaf-blindness require?

      a) _____

      b) _____

C. Autism
   1. What six characteristics are frequently observed in children with autism?

      a) _____

      b) _____

      c) _____

      d) _____

      e) _____

      f) _____

III. Prevalence
   A. Why are there no uniform figures on prevalence for severe disabilities?

      1. _____

   B. What is the estimated prevalence of severe disabilities?

      1. _____ percent of the population

IV. Causes of Severe Disabilities
   A. What are the causes of severe disabilities?

      1. _____

      2. _____

      3. _____

      4. _____

V. Educational Approaches
   A. What three questions must be considered to determine how to teach children with severe disabilities?

      1. _____

      2. _____

      3. _____

   B. Curriculum
      1. Contemporary curriculum content is characterized by:

         a) _____

      2. Functional skills are:

         a) _____

         b) _____

         c) _____

         d) _____

      3. Why is it necessary to teach chronological age-appropriate skills?

         a) _____

         b) _____

         c) _____

      4. Why is it important to teach choice-making skills?

         a) _____

      5. Communication Skills
         a) What two changes in perspective regarding the nature of communication are shaping contemporary research and instruction for people with severe disabilities?

            1) _____

            2) _____

         b) How do we know if communication is functional?

            1) _____

                _____

6. Facilitated Communication
   a) What is facilitated communication?

       1) _____

           _____

   b) What has the research on facilitated communication demonstrated?

       1) _____

       2) _____

7. How can teaching appropriate recreation and leisure skills help individuals with severe disabilities?

   a) _____

   b) _____

   c) _____

8. How should instructional targets be prioritized and selected?

   a) _____

C. Instructional Methods
   1. Careful attention should be given to the following components of an instructional program for students with severe disabilities:

   a) _____

   b) _____

   c) _____

   d) _____

   e) _____

   f) _____

   2. Partial Participation
   a) How can partial participation help the learner?

       1) _____

       2) _____

       3) _____

b)   What are four types of misapplications of partial participation?

1)   _____

2)   _____

3)   _____

4)   _____

3.   Positive Behavioral Support
   a)   A growing number of special education programs are responding to challenging, excessive, or unacceptable behaviors by attempting to:

1)   _____

2)   _____

3)   _____

4)   _____

   b)   What are the three steps of functional assessment?

1)   _____

2)   _____

3)   _____

   c)   Problem behaviors such as noncompliance, aggression, acting out, and self-injury can be reduced by using what types of instructional modifications?

1)   _____

2)   _____

3)   _____

4)   _____

5)   _____

4.   What are the advantages of small group instruction?

a)   _____

b)   _____

c)   _____

d)   _____

D. Where Should Students with Severe Disabilities Be Taught?
    1. What are the benefits of the neighborhood school?

        a) _____

        b) _____

        c) _____

        d) _____

    2. What are strategies for promoting social relationships?

        a) _____

        b) _____

    3. Experiences and Transformations of General Education Teachers
        a) What are the three roles of an effective inclusion facilitator?

            1) _____

            2) _____

            3) _____

    4. How Much Time in the Regular Classroom?
        a) What is a major challenge for general and special educators?

            1) _____

                _____

E. The Challenge and Rewards of Teaching Students with Severe Disabilities
    1. What are important characteristics for a teacher of students with severe disabilities?

        a) _____

        b) _____

        c) _____

        d) _____

        e) _____

CHAPTER THIRTEEN
SEVERE DISABILITIES

Objectives

1. State the various definitions of severe disabilities.

2. Identify the characteristics of individuals with severe disabilities.

3. Explain the basic instructional approaches for children with dual sensory impairments.

4. Describe the characteristics of children with autism.

5. State the estimated prevalence of students with severe disabilities.

6. Describe the causes of severe disabilities.

7. Describe the types of skills that are most appropriate to teach children with severe disabilities.

8. Explain the types of augmentative and alternative communication used by children with severe disabilities.

9. Discuss the research findings on the use of facilitated communication.

10. Describe the elements of effective instruction for students with severe disabilities.

11. Describe the traits a teacher must possess to effectively work with students with severe disabilities.

Self-check Quiz

1. A recent realization in the field of severe disabilities is that individuals with severe disabilities:
   a. cannot learn.
   b. are more retarded than they were first thought to be.
   c. can and do learn.
   d. can be cured.

2. The prevailing philosophy regarding the education of students with severe disabilities is one of:
   a. inclusion.
   b. exclusion.
   c. love and dedication.
   d. pessimism.

3. Which approach defines individuals with severe disabilities as "those individuals age 21 and younger who are functioning at a level half or less than the level which would be expected on the basis of chronological age"?
   a. behavioral
   b. psychodynamic
   c. ecological
   d. developmental

4. Which of the following is NOT one of the six frequently observed characteristics of children with autism identified by Lovaas and Newsom (1976)?
   a. self-stimulation
   b. above average intellectual functioning
   c. tantrums
   d. severe affect isolation

5. The basic skills definition of severe disabilities:
   a. makes it clear that education of students with severe disabilities must not focus on traditional academic instruction.
   b. states that developmental levels should be emphasized when providing instruction.
   c. states that a student with severe disabilities is one who needs instruction in basic skills such as decoding words, adding numbers, and writing sentences.
   d. all of the above

6. Which of the following activities would not be chronologically age-appropriate for a 17-year-old girl with severe disabilities?
   a. squeezing a rubber toy to improve coordination and motor control
   b. learning to fold laundry
   c. learning to play rock music on a tape recorder
   d. learning to bowl

7. Juan, a 14-year-old student with severe disabilities, is just learning to feed himself. Which of the following strategies should be used in teaching Juan to eat independently?
   a. A developmental approach should provide the basis for teaching.
   b. Juan should be taught to feed himself exactly the way a nondisabled 2-year-old would be taught.
   c. Juan should be taught using the same materials one would use with a nondisabled 2-year-old.
   d. none of the above

8. Communication boards, symbol systems, and sign language are examples of:
   a. augmentative communication systems.
   b. transitional communication.
   c. facilitated communication.
   d. simulated language.

9. Which of the following statements best describes the work potential of students with severe disabilities?
   a. Because of their severe disabilities, these students do not have the potential for useful, remunerative work.
   b. These students may be able to work in sheltered workshops, but community employment is unrealistic.
   c. Given the right training and support, these students have the potential for productive and meaningful work in a wide variety of settings.
   d. Although some of these students might be able to work in a community setting, they would receive greater wages and benefits if they were employed in a sheltered workshop.

10. Ms. Hopper, a teacher of students with severe disabilities, took her students to a fast food restaurant. Which of the following procedures would be the best way for Ms. Hopper to help her students order?
    a. To save time, she should order hamburgers and drinks for all of the students.
    b. She should present the students with two or three pictures of sandwich choices and two or three pictures of drink choices and let them indicate their choices.
    c. She should ask the waitress to bring the students the restaurant's most popular sandwich and drink.
    d. Before going to the restaurant, she should find out from students' parents what they like and order what the parents suggest.

11. The development of appropriate recreation and leisure skills is considered important for students with severe disabilities because these skills can help them:
    a. interact socially.
    b. maintain their physical skills.
    c. become more involved in community activities.
    d. all of the above

12. The TASH definition of individuals with severe disabilities refers to the:
    a. level of support needed by these individuals.
    b. duration of support needed by these individuals.
    c. focus of support needed by these individuals.
    d. all of the above

13. Current treatment of the excessive or unacceptable behavior of students with severe disabilities focuses on the use of:
    a. strategies that have been validated and intended for use in integrated community settings.
    b. validated aversive techniques.
    c. extended time-out procedures.
    d. interventions that would be unacceptable if used with individuals who do not have disabilities.

14. Mrs. Figueroa, the mother of a student with severe disabilities, indicated to her son's teacher that she wanted him to learn to feed himself. After agreeing that this was an appropriate goal, the teacher assessed the student's current level of feeding-related skills and abilities. What should the teacher do next?
    a. Determine what reinforcement to use with the student.
    b. Promote generalization of the student's learning.
    c. Clearly define the specific skill to be taught.
    d. Decide how long instruction should last.

15. Which of the following skills would be most functional for a student with severe disabilities?
    a. improving eye hand coordination by stringing beads
    b. experiencing different tactile sensations by tracing the alphabet on letters cut from sandpaper
    c. showing a card to a bus driver that contains the student's name and address
    d. all of the above

CHAPTER FOURTEEN
GIFTEDNESS AND TALENT DEVELOPMENT

Focus Questions

- **Why do students who are very bright need special education?**

Special education is necessary for children when their physical attributes and/or learning abilities differ from the norm to such an extent that an individualized program of special education is required to meet their needs. When a traditional classroom curriculum is not allowing children who are gifted and talented to fulfill their potential and to succeed fully in school, then special education is needed.

- **How has the evolving definition of giftedness changed the ways in which students are identified and served?**

Intelligence, creativity, and talent have been central to the various definitions that have been proposed over the years, and they continue to be reflected in the current and still-evolving definitions. Historically, however, the concept of giftedness has been neither as broad nor as inclusive as the definitions we currently use. According to most early definitions, only those individuals with outstanding performances on standard intelligence tests were considered gifted. This narrow view of giftedness dominated by an IQ score prevailed for many years and came to be associated with only the Caucasian, urban, middle-and upper-class segments of society. In the early 1950s, J.P. Guilford, a psychologist, challenged the field to look beyond traditional conceptions of intelligence and to view the IQ score as a small sample of mental abilities. Current definitions have grown out of our awareness that IQ alone does not define all the possible areas of giftedness. Today's definitions include many talents that contribute substantially to the quality of life for both the individual and society. This more comprehensive definition allows us to identify and serve a more diverse group of gifted learners.

- **What provisions should be made to accurately identify students with outstanding talents who are from diverse cultural groups or have disabilities?**

Today more so than ever, we recognize the need for culturally non-biased identification and assessment practices. Current "best practices" for identifying these students from diverse cultural groups involves a multifactored assessment process. Maker (1994) developed a procedure called DISCOVER that is used to assess gifted students from diverse backgrounds, female students, and students with disabilities. The DISCOVER assessment process involves a series of five progressively more complex problems that provide children with various ways to demonstrate problem-solving competence with the content and with one another.

- **How can the regular classroom teacher provide instruction at the pace and depth needed by gifted and talented students while at the same time meeting the needs of other students in the classroom?**

Three common approaches to educating students who are gifted and talented are curriculum compacting, enrichment, and acceleration. Each of these approaches can be used by the regular classroom teacher. Some experts (Feldhusen & Moon, 1995) advocate the development of an individualized growth plan to develop a broad program of services for gifted and talented students. The growth plan should include assessment information, student-generated goals, and the recommended activities for accomplishing these goals. A key ingredient of this approach is that the student is an active participant in all instructional and evaluative activities. Similar to the IEP, a growth plan could be used to guide the teacher in the development of appropriate lessons for the gifted and talented while at the same time meeting the needs of the other students. In addition, recent advancement in technology could be used to help further individualize the gifted student's program.

- **Should gifted students be educated with their same-age peers or with older students who share the same intellectual and academic talents and interests?**

Students' individual needs, both academic and social, must guide the selection of the most appropriate educational environment for these students. The overall goal of educational programs for students who are gifted and talented should be the fullest possible development of each child's actual and potential abilities. For some children who are gifted and talented, education with older students will be appropriate while for others education with same age peers will be appropriate. Review the research on acceleration to assist you in responding to this question.

Chapter Overview

Your study of exceptional children thus far has focused on students with intellectual, behavioral, or physical disabilities—children who require specially tailored programs of education in order to benefit from education. Gifted and talented children represent the other end on the continuum of academic, artistic, social, and scientific abilities. Just as the traditional curriculum is often inappropriate for the child with a disability, it also can be inappropriate for the child who is gifted and talented. The traditional curriculum may not provide the kinds of challenges the student who is gifted and talented requires to learn most effectively. As a result, these students may represent the most underserved group of exceptional children.

Numerous definitions of gifted and talented children have been proposed and debated over the years. This chapter presents the evolution of the definition currently in use. Historically the concept of giftedness has been neither as broad nor as inclusive as the definitions currently in use. Schools must develop a system to identify students who are gifted and talented that (a) seeks variety, (b) uses many assessment measures, (c) is free of bias, (d) is fluid (accommodates students who develop at different rates and whose interests may change as they mature), (e) identifies potential, and (f) assesses motivation.

In the broadest sense, the overall goals of education programs for children who are gifted and talented are no different from the goals of education for all children—feelings of self-worth, self-sufficiency, civic responsibility, and vocational and avocational competence. How schools meet these educational goals varies from district to district and from classroom to classroom. Three common educational approaches are: enrichment, curriculum compacting, and acceleration. Enrichment experiences are those that let students investigate topics of interest in much greater detail than is ordinarily possible with the standard school curriculum. Curriculum compacting is compressing the instructional content and materials so that academically able students have more time to work on more challenging materials. Acceleration is the general term for modifying the pace at which the student moves through the curriculum (e.g., early admission to school, grade skipping, testing out of courses). For some students with outstanding talents, the things that take place outside of the classroom may be more important and rewarding than many of the things that take place inside the classroom. The options for learning outside include (a) special courses offered by educational agencies, and (b) community-based learning opportunities.

If the long-range needs of the society are to be met, it must capitalize on one of its most precious human resources—children who are gifted and talented. Given the opportunities to reach their potential, many of these children will contribute to the quality of our collective future. Of more immediate concern, and perhaps even more importantly, the educational needs of these exceptional children must be met because they are deserving of an appropriate education.

CHAPTER FOURTEEN AT A GLANCE

MAIN TOPICS	KEY POINTS	KEY TERMS	MARGIN NOTES
Defining Giftedness and Talent	• The federal government defines gifted and talented children as exhibiting high performance capability in intellectual, creative, and/or artistic areas, possessing an unusual leadership capacity, or excelling in specific academic fields. • Renzulli's definition of giftedness is based on the traits of above-average general abilities, high level of task commitment, and creativity. • Feldhusen's definition of giftedness emphasizes talent as the primary defining characteristic. • Piirto defines the gifted as having superior memory, observational powers, curiosity, creativity, and ability to learn. • Maker defines the gifted and talented student as a problem solver who is capable of (a) creating a new or more clear definition of an existing problem, (b) devising new and more efficient or effective methods, and (c) reaching solutions that may be different from the usual.	• general intellectual ability • specific academic aptitude • talent • paradigm • gifted • outstanding talent • exceptional talent	• *Psychomotor ability*—high performance in gross and fine motor development—was included as a sixth area of giftedness in an earlier federal definition (P.L. 91-230). However, Congress believed that schools' existing athletic programs serve such students adequately. • A *paradigm* is an overall model or view of a concept or phenomenon.
Characteristics of Students Who Are Gifted and Talented	• Learning and intellectual characteristics of gifted and talented students include the ability to: • Rapidly acquire, retain, and use large amounts of information • Relate one idea to another	• interindividual • intraindividual • asynchronous development	• The ability to manipulate symbol systems is a key indicator of intellectual giftedness. Although the most common symbol system is language, there are numerous other symbol systems, such as scientific notation, music and dance notation, mathematics, and engineering symbols. These

systems can be incorporated into creative endeavors as well as academic and intellectual areas.

- Most highly gifted children experience *asynchronous development*, in which mental, physical, emotional, and social development occur at dramatically different rates. Their cognitive and intellectual abilities usually outpace their physical development.
- Gifted and talented children are most often identified by creativity, talent, and/or extreme intellectual ability that is atypical for their age.

- Make sound judgments
- Perceive the operation of larger systems of knowledge that may not be recognized by the ordinary citizen
- Acquire and manipulate abstract symbol systems
- Solve problems by reframing the question and creating novel solutions
- Gifted children are by no means perfect, and their unusual talents and abilities may make them either withdrawn or difficult to manage in the classroom.
- Gifted students need both basic and advanced content knowledge and the abilities to use and develop that knowledge effectively.
- Many gifted children are creative. Although there is no universally accepted definition of creativity, we know that creative children have knowledge, examine it in a variety of ways, critically analyze the outcomes, and communicate their ideas.
- Guilford includes dimensions of fluency, flexibility, originality, and elaboration in his definition of creativity.

- This feature presents a multiple-choice format in which the reader must identify the authors of specific statements.

Profiles & Perspectives: Making the Earth a Better Place

	Key terms	Details
Profiles & Perspectives: Precocity as a Hallmark of Giftedness		• Underachievement is the prevailing situation in the education of academically talented young children in most schools today. The main way to recognize talented students is by predictive behaviors or their precocity: achievements resembling those of older children.
Prevalence	• social construct	• The most commonly cited prevalence estimate is that gifted students make up about 3% to 5% of the school-age population. • There is no "correct" prevalence of gifted and talented children. Because giftedness is a social construct, there are as many gifted and talented students as the definition in use determines. • States are not required to provide special services to gifted and talented students or to report the number of children served, although they are required to do so for children with disabilities.
Identification and Assessment	• precocity	• IQ tests are the initial, but not necessarily the best, means for identifying students with intellectual high ability. • The usual means of identification include a combination of IQ scores; creativity and achievement measures; teacher, parent, and peer nominations; and self-nomination. • Maker's DISCOVER procedure can be used to identify gifted and talented students from diverse cultural groups and females in an equitable fashion. • "We can find outstanding talent by observing students at work in rich and varied educational settings. Providing opportunities and observing performance give the best information on children's strengths" (U. S. Department of Education, 1993, pp. 25–26). • A national survey found that 73% of school districts use the IQ and achievement tests as the primary tools for identifying the only category of gifted student that they serve: students with high general intelligence (U.S. Department of Education, 1993).

Topic	Key Terms	Content
		• Howard Gardner's theory of multiple intelligences (1983, 1996) proposes an expanded definition of intelligence that entails eight separate domains—linguistic, musical, logical-mathematical, spatial, bodily-kinesthetic, interpersonal, intrapersonal, and naturalist—that operate somewhat independently of one another but that interact at other levels when a person in engaged in active problem solving.	• The finding of one national survey that teachers usually make only minor, if any, changes in curricular content for gifted students is not encouraging in this respect (Archambault et al., 1993). In a related study, the same researchers found that in more than 84% of the instructional activities, gifted and talented children were not provided with any meaningful instructional or curricular differentiation (Westberg, Archambault, Dobyns, & Slavin, 1993). • Technology can be used to provide both acceleration and enrichment opportunities for gifted students. • Teachers must avoid the temptation and ease of providing gifted students the MOTS curriculum (More of The Same)—repetitious and unnecessary drill and practice of the same kinds of items or problems the students have already mastered. MOTS activities may be one reason that some students underachieve (Clark, 1997).
Profiles & Perspectives: I Was Thinking About Black Holes		• Teachers and parents can foster the intellectual and talent development of children with disabilities by conveying positive, realistic expectations; encouraging independence; guiding constructive coping strategies; providing daily opportunities to build abilities and enjoy success; and pursuing positive social experiences for the child. • World-famous theoretical physicist Stephen W. Hawking talks about his views of the Big Bang singularity and quantum mechanics.	
Educational Approaches	• qualitatively different • acceleration • enrichment • acceleration • curriculum compacting • enrichment • saturated learning environment	• Three common approaches to educating gifted and talented students are acceleration, curriculum compacting, and enrichment. • Four models for teaching gifted students are: Renzulli's Schoolwide Enrichment Triad Model, Clark's Responsive Learning Environment, Maker's Active Problem Solver Model, and Betts's Autonomous Learner Model.	
Profiles & Perspectives: Dumbing Down: Pretending That All Students Are Equal Doesn't Make It So		• The national ambivalence about ability is it's okay to extol athletic excellence, but there's something elitist, or at least unseemly, about even acknowledging intellectual excellence.	

	• What's more important for gifted and talented students—acceleration or enrichment? "The question of acceleration versus enrichment is irrelevant, because this group of students needs both. They learn at a very accelerated pace, and they need high-level conceptual material outside the regular curriculum" (Silverman, 1995, p. 229).
Teaching & Learning in School: New and Emerging Technologies for Gifted and Talented Students	• The identification of appropriate software for a gifted student is dependent on the curricular goals for a particular student. New and emerging technologies for gifted and talented students are intelligent computer-assisted-instruction (ICAI), virtual reality, and electronic communities.
Current Issues and Future Trends	• The conceptual and definitional nature of "giftedness" is being more intensively questioned. • The likely possibility is that most services for gifted and talented students will originate from the regular teacher within the regular classroom. • The importance of identifying gifted and talented students among females, individuals with disabilities, and diverse cultural groups is now being recognized. We need better procedures for identifying, assessing, teaching, and encouraging these children. • As we have seen with other exceptional children, we must improve society's attitudes toward gifted and talented children if we are to improve their futures.

CHAPTER FOURTEEN
GIFTEDNESS AND TALENT DEVELOPMENT

Guided Review

I.   Defining Giftedness and Talent
  A. Federal Definition
    1. According to the Gifted and Talented Act of 1978, gifted and talented children are those possessing demonstrated or potential abilities that give evidence of high performance capability in which areas?

       a) _____

       b) _____

       c) _____

       d) _____

  B. An Emerging Paradigm: From Intelligence to Talent
    1. Feldhusen describes an emerging paradigm of giftedness that emphasizes:

       a) _____

  C. What are the three clusters of human traits in Renzuli's three-trait definition?

    1. _____

    2. _____

    3. _____

  D. Piirto defines gifted individuals as those who possess what characteristics?

    1. _____

    2. _____

    3. _____

    4. _____

    5. _____

E. Maker's Problem-solving Perspective
   1. Creative problem solvers are capable of:

   a) _____

   b) _____

   c) _____

F. New Definition of Outstanding Talent
   1. Schools must develop a system to identify gifted and talented students that:

   a) _____

   b) _____

   c) _____

   d) _____

   e) _____

   f) _____

II. Characteristics of Students Who Are Gifted and Talented
   A. What are the characteristics of gifted and talented students?

   1. _____

   2. _____

   3. _____

   4. _____

   5. _____

   6. _____

   B. What are the characteristics of highly gifted children (Silverman, 1995)?

   1. _____

   2. _____

   3. _____

   4. _____

   5. _____

   6. _____

7. _____

8. _____

C. Creativity
   1. What are the dimensions of creative behavior (Guilford, 1987)?

      a) _____

      b) _____

      c) _____

      d) _____

      e) _____

      f) _____

      g) _____

      h) _____

   2. What are the ten characteristics of highly creative people (Torrance, 1993)?

      a) _____

      b) _____

      c) _____

      d) _____

      e) _____

      f) _____

      g) _____

      h) _____

      i) _____

      j) _____

III. Prevalence
   A. According to the Marland Report, what percentage of the school-age population is gifted?

      1. _____

B. If we include students who are highly talented, what is the estimated prevalence?

    1. _____

C. How many states have gifted programs?

    1. _____

D. How many students are currently being served?

    1. _____

IV. Identification and Assessment
    A. What six basic principles must be taken into account when identifying gifted students?

        1. _____

        2. _____

        3. _____

        4. _____

        5. _____

        6. _____

    B. A multifactored assessment approach should use information from what sources?

        1. _____

        2. _____

        3. _____

        4. _____

        5. _____

        6. _____

        7. _____

        8. _____

    C. Multicultural Assessment and Identification
        1. Current best practices for identifying gifted and talented students from diverse cultural groups involve a multifactored assessment process that meets what criteria?

            a) _____

            b) _____

c) _____

d) _____

e) _____

f) _____

g) _____

2. What is the DISCOVER procedure?

   a) _____

   b) Use of the DISCOVER model with culturally diverse students produced the following results:

      1) _____

         _____

      2) _____

         _____

      3) _____

         _____

      4) _____

         _____

D. Gifted and Talented Girls
   1. What are the key issues concerning the identification of girls?

      a) _____

      b) _____

      c) _____

      d) _____

   2. Programs serving gifted and talented females should strive to:

      a) _____

      b) _____

      c) _____

      d) _____

E. Gifted and Talented Students with Disabilities
   1. What specific recommendations have been made for developing school programs for students who are gifted and learning disabled?

   a) _____

   b) _____

   c) _____

   d) _____

   e) _____

V. Educational Approaches
   A. Curricular Goals
      1. What should the differentiated curriculum do?

      a) _____

      b) _____

      c) _____

      d) _____

      e) _____

   B. What characteristics of the curriculum and instruction does Piirto recommend?

      1. _____

      2. _____

      3. _____

   C. Curriculum Organization and Delivery Methods
      1. What are examples of acceleration?

      a) _____

      b) _____

      c) _____

      d) _____

      e) _____

      f) _____

g) _____

h) _____

2. What is curriculum compacting?

    a) _____

    _____

3. What is enrichment?

    a) _____

    _____

4. What are suggestions for curriculum differentiation outside the classroom?

    a) _____

    b) _____

    c) _____

    d) _____

    e) _____

    f) _____

D. Instructional Models and Methods
    1. What are the relevant features of the schoolwide enrichment model?

    a) _____

    b) _____

    c) _____

    2. What are the characteristics of the responsive learning environment?

    a) _____

    b) _____

    c) _____

    d) _____

    e) _____

f) _____

g) _____

3. What are the components of Maker's active problem solving model?

   a) _____

   b) _____

   c) _____

   d) _____

4. What are the five dimensions of the autonomous learner model?

   a) _____

   b) _____

   c) _____

   d) _____

   e) _____

VI. What Are the Current Issues and Future Trends of Gifted Education?

   A. _____

   B. _____

   C. _____

   D. _____

CHAPTER FOURTEEN
GIFTEDNESS AND TALENT DEVELOPMENT

Objectives

1. Explain the various definitions of *gifted* and *talented*.

2. Describe the characteristics of children who are gifted and talented.

3. Identify the prevalence of gifted and talented children.

4. Describe how gifted and talented children are typically identified.

5. Explain alternative assessment techniques for identifying gifted students from diverse backgrounds.

6. Describe how teachers can foster the intellectual and talent development of gifted children with disabilities.

7. Explain what is meant by *acceleration*, *curriculum compacting*, and *enrichment*.

8. Describe the various models used for teaching gifted and talented students.

9. Describe the future trends of assessment and instruction for gifted and talented students.

Self-check Quiz

1. According to the Gifted and Talented Act of 1978, gifted and talented children are individuals:
   a. with high standards for themselves.
   b. possessing demonstrated or potential abilities that give evidence of high performance capabilities who need services not ordinarily provided by the school.
   c. showing potential in the performing or visual arts who need services not ordinarily provided by the school.
   d. both b & c

2. Chandra performs exceptionally well in math and science; however, her abilities in the language arts are about the same as most of her same-age peers. Chandra's performance:
   a. demonstrates general intellectual ability.
   b. demonstrates specific academic aptitude.
   c. does not fit the definition of gifted and talented.
   d. both a & b

3. Renzuli's definition of gifted uses all of the following except:
   a. outstanding problem-solving skills.
   b. above average intellectual abilities.
   c. a high level of task commitment.
   d. creativity.

4. Gifted and talented children comprise approximately _____ of the school-age population.
   a. 5-10%
   b. 10-15%
   c. 15-20%
   d. 20-30%

5. Which of the following is NOT a characteristic of highly gifted children, according to Silverman (1995)?
   a. intense intellectual curiosity
   b. perfectionism
   c. tendency towards extroversion
   d. early moral and existential concern

6. Creativity is:
   a. not central to the definition of giftedness.
   b. the highest form of giftedness.
   c. not universally defined.
   d. b & c

7. The most critical component for identifying a gifted and talented student is:
   a. developing a profile of the student.
   b. having someone notice exceptional abilities in the student.
   c. the administration and analysis of achievement and intelligence tests.
   d. a functional assessment.

8. Which of the following populations are likely to perform at a less than desirable level on standard forms of intelligence testing?
   a. individuals with disabilities
   b. Hispanic-Americans
   c. females
   d. all of the above

9. In a creativity measure, Sancho is given one minute to list as many uses for a paper clip as he can. Which dimension of creativity is being assessed?
   a. convergent thinking
   b. flexibility
   c. fluency
   d. originality

10. Mr. Esperanza gives Kevin extended assignments within the regular curriculum such as situational role plays, additional readings, and problem-based learning. Which of the following educational approaches is being implemented?
    a. enrichment
    b. curriculum compacting
    c. a pull-out model
    d. acceleration

11. One example of the acceleration approach is:
    a. giving students more challenging work to keep them going at the same pace as their peers.
    b. giving students a larger quantity of work to keep them going at the same pace as their peers.
    c. allowing students to work at a more rapid pace through the same curriculum.
    d. teaching students special techniques to increase their rate of learning, such as problem solving shortcuts or speed reading.

12. Which of the following is an example of the enrichment approach?
    a. concurrent enrollment in both high school and college
    b. grade skipping
    c. curriculum compacting
    d. none of the above

13. Which of the following activities would require MORE divergent than convergent thinking?
    a. matching identical shapes
    b. classification of objects into groups of likeness
    c. write as many correct number problems as you can which equal 10
    d. name the objects on a table

14. Studies of instructional accommodations for gifted and talented students indicate that general education teachers:
    a. modify the curriculum for gifted and talented students.
    b. make differentiated assignments for gifted and talented students.
    c. provide specialized opportunities for gifted and talented students.
    d. none of the above

15. One of the pressing challenges in the education of gifted and talented students is:
    a. the addition of counseling services for these individuals.
    b. the addition of social skill instruction for these individuals.
    c. the development of appropriate curriculum models and instructional strategies for these individuals.
    d. finding the resources to develop more specialized classes for these individuals.

CHAPTER FIFTEEN
TRANSITION TO ADULTHOOD

Focus Questions

- **How can special education programs for school-age children with disabilities prepare them for successful transition to life as adults?**

  Clark and Kolstoe have developed a model that focuses on obtaining work after one leaves school but gives equal importance to competencies that are critical for life as an adult. There are four mutually important elements of the model: (a) values, attitudes, and habits; (b) human relationships; (c) occupational information; and (d) acquisition of job and daily living skills. The relative emphasis of the four elements changes as a student progresses through the elementary and middle school grades and moves into high school and postsecondary education or vocational training opportunities and as individual needs and career goals change.

- **What are the most appropriate and effective programs and services for supporting adults with disabilities in their efforts to find and keep meaningful work, to locate a home, or to use community recreation centers?**

  The role of the employment specialist/job coach is evolving from one of primary supporter for the employee with disabilities to one who works with the employer and co-workers to help identify, develop, and facilitate the typical or indigenous support of the workplace. Increased community-based residential services have meant a greater opportunity for adults with severe disabilities to live in a more normalized setting. Three residential alternatives for adults with mental retardation and related developmental disabilities—group homes, foster homes, and apartment living—help complete a continuum of possible living arrangements between the highly structured and typically segregated public institution and fully independent living. Special educators must realize the importance of including training for recreation and leisure in curricula for school-age children with disabilities. Learning appropriate leisure skills is particularly important for adults with severe disabilities.

- **How can services such as sheltered employment programs, which are designed and intended to help adults with disabilities, also limit their participation in life activities?**

  In the process of creating teaching and working environments that promote success for individuals with disabilities, we sometimes fail to adequately prepare them to live and work in more normalized settings. How? We create teaching and learning environments that are significantly different than more normalized settings, thereby limiting opportunities to participate in more normalized settings. As a result, attempts at integration into normalized settings are unsuccessful. Even though all individuals with disabilities will not likely achieve full independence in their communities, special education must plan its instruction to provide every opportunity for the achievement of independent adult living by individuals with disabilities.

- **Does it make sense for society to provide the ongoing supports a person with severe disabilities needs to work and live in the community?**

  There are two basic reasons why such support makes sense. First, individuals with disabilities have a fundamental right to live and participate independently, to the greatest extent possible, in normalized settings and programs. Nondisabled individuals have the responsibility to help individuals with disabilities to obtain these rights. Second, when individuals with severe disabilities do not become self-sufficient, contributing members of their communities, others are left with the responsibility of providing lifelong custodial care.

- **Why must quality of life be the ultimate outcome measure for special education?**

If all the educational programs, employment opportunities, and residential services do not contribute to an improved lifestyle for individuals with disabilities, little has been accomplished. A person may have been taught many skills, but if those skills do not enable her to enjoy the benefits available in personal, social, work, and leisure settings, the wrong skills have been taught and a disservice has been done to that individual.

Chapter Overview _____

Children often imagine that life as an adult will be easy. After all, adults seem to have more answers than questions. Most young people entering adulthood are in for a bit of a surprise, however. Things aren't quite as simple as they appeared. Imagine what it must be like for an adult with severe disabilities when he or she is faced with the challenges of adulthood. Many exceptional children have not been prepared for "life-after-special education." In addition, many adults with disabilities are afforded only a limited number of lifestyle choices because of prevailing prejudices and misconceptions about them.

The quality of life for most adults with disabilities in the mid-1990s is better than it has ever been. Over the past 25 years, adults with mental retardation have been moving from large institutions into smaller, more normalized, community-based living environments. Increasingly, these adults are employed in integrated settings. Special education has come a long way in educating exceptional children to be better prepared for the challenges and joys of being an adult. In addition, society at large is providing more of the same opportunities to these adults. There, however, remains much work to be done.

Because so many professionals have dedicated themselves to learning more about effective programming for transition into adulthood, there are more exceptional adults than ever working, living, and enjoying leisure activities in community-based, integrated settings. In the not too distant past, the opportunity for adults with disabilities to earn competitive wages for meaningful work was almost nonexistent. Today, a type of vocational opportunity referred to as supported employment enables individuals with severe disabilities to participate successfully in integrated settings. Several supported employment models are described in detail in this chapter.

Increased community-based residential services for adults with disabilities provide a greater opportunity for them to live in more normalized settings. Three residential alternatives for adults with mental retardation and related developmental disabilities—group homes, foster homes, and semi-independent apartment living—help to complete the continuum of possible living arrangements between the segregated, public institution and fully independent living. The advantages of each of these living options are described, as well as outcomes of and issues related to community-based living for adults with disabilities.

In addition to educating individuals with disabilities in work and independent-living skills, many professionals realize the importance of teaching recreation and leisure skills. Learning appropriate recreational and leisure-time activities is difficult for many adults with disabilities. The chapter discusses several leisure-time and therapeutic recreation programs.

There is a long way to go in developing effective transition-to-adulthood programming and in improving society's attitudes toward the integration of adults with disabilities into work, residential, and recreational settings. The accomplishments in the recent past give reason for optimism that transitional services will continue to grow and improve.

CHAPTER FIFTEEN AT A GLANCE

MAIN TOPICS	KEY POINTS	KEY TERMS	MARGIN NOTES
How Do Former Special Education Students Fare as Adults?	• Data from the National Longitudinal Transition Study (NLTS) show an unemployment rate of 46% for all youth with disabilities who have been out of school for less than two years; most of the young adults who had found competitive employment were working in part-time, low-paying jobs. • The unemployment rate for young adults with disabilities drops to 36.5% when they have been out of school for three to five years, but nearly one in five (19.6%) states she has given up looking for work (NTLS). • Only 58% of teenagers and young adults with disabilities who exited from the public schools during the 1991-92 school year graduated with a diploma or received a certificate of completion, and it is estimated that 30% of students with disabilities who enroll in high school drop out before they finish. • Although the percentage of college students who indicate they have a disability has increased in recent years, compared to their peers without disabilities, fewer former special education students pursue postsecondary education. • NLTS reported that four out of every five former special education students have still not achieved the status of independent adulthood after being out of high school for up to five years.	• follow-up studies • follow-along studies	• A *follow-up study* collects information at a single point in time and shows a "snapshot" of adult adjustment. A *follow-along study* collects information on postschool outcomes at multiple points in time and enables the assessment of progress over time (Darrow & Clark, 1992). • NLTS is an ongoing effort to assess and monitor changes in the adult adjustment of youth with disabilities after they leave secondary special education programs. NLTS has tracked more than 8,000 youths with disabilities who left U.S. secondary special education programs between 1985 and 1987. • The percentage of first-time, full-time freshmen enrolled in college who indicate they have a disability has increased significantly in recent years (Henderson, 1992). The majority are students with learning disabilities. • Requirements for graduation and the type of exit document for students with disabilities vary tremendously from state to state (Thurlow, Ysseldyke, and Reid, 1997). • The case studies of four young adults with learning disabilities who had dropped out of high school "cast doubt on the prevailing opinion that school dropouts are 'losers' and 'failures'" (Lichtenstein, 1993, p. 336). Their personal stories reveal both the shortfalls and inadequacies of the secondary special education and transition services they had received and the "considerable resiliency" in the former students' efforts to seek out jobs, develop friendships, gain alternative education credentials, and pursue career ambitions.

251

Teaching & Learning: A Friendship Program for Future Special Education Teachers	Students enrolled in a college level course about special education were paired with and got to know on a personal basis an adult with developmental disabilities living in a group home, family home, or supported living apartment. Student insights were that the adults with developmental disabilities lacked social skills, money-handling skills, and self-care skills.	It is important to note that the very small percentage of young adults who met the criteria for "successful" transition to adult life in this study had *graduated* from secondary special education programs. Young adults who leave secondary programs by routes other than graduation do not fare as well as those who do complete school with a diploma or certificate (Blackorby & Wagner, 1996; Malian & Love, 1998). Participating in community recreation and leisure activities with an adult with disabilities is an excellent way to appreciate the importance of a functional curriculum for school-age students.
Transition from School to Adult Life: Models and Services	Transition from school to life in the community has become perhaps the most challenging issue in special education today. Models for school to adult-life transition stress the importance of a functional secondary-school curriculum that provides work experience in integrated community job sites, systematic coordination between the school and adult service agencies, parental involvement and support, and a written individualized transition plan (ITP) to guide the entire process. Development of career awareness and vocational skills should begin in the elementary grades for children with severe disabilities. Middle school students should begin to spend time on actual community job sites.	supported employment individualized transition plan (ITP) individual rehabilitation plan individualized habilitation plan Brolin's *Life-Centered Career Education* (1997) is an excellent career education curriculum. Project WORK is a field-tested classroom-based employability skills curriculum designed to place students in jobs in six weeks (Patton, de la Graza, & Harmon, 1997).

Topic	Key Points	Key Terms	Research
Profiles & Perspectives: Removing Transition Hurdles with Effective Communication	• Secondary students should spend more time on actual community job sites, with in-school instruction focusing on the functional skills needed in the adult world, domestic, community, and recreational/leisure environments. • With supports and effective communication among service providers and the family, an adult with disabilities can transition to independence. It is important for teachers to be flexible and creative when trying to provide community job sites.		
Employment	• Secondary school programs can enhance the competitive employment prospects for young adults with disabilities by (1) stressing functional, vocational skills; (2) conducting school-based instruction in integrated settings as much as possible; and (3) beginning community-based instruction as early as about age 12 for students with severe disabilities and for progressively extended periods as the student nears graduation. • Supported employment is a relatively new concept that recognizes that many adults with severe disabilities require ongoing support to obtain and hold a job. Supported employment is characterized by performance of real paid work in regular, integrated work sites; it requires ongoing support from a supported work specialist.	• work • competitive employment • supported employment • integrated work setting • work enclave • mobile work crew • small business enterprise model • natural support • sheltered workshop • work activity center contracting • prime manufacturing reclamation	• Several follow-up studies have found a positive correlation between paid work experiences during high school and postschool employment (e.g., Benz, Yovanoff, & Doren, 1997; D'Amico, 1991; Hasazi, Gordon, & Roe, 1985; Hasazi, Johnson, Hasazi, Gordon, & Hull, 1989; Kohler, 1994; Scuccimarra & Speece, 1990). The NLTS, however, found that only 39% of young adults with disabilities had been enrolled in work experience programs during high school. • An *integrated work setting* requires contact with nondisabled co-workers. • The individual placement (job coach) model is the most widely used supported employment approach (79.7%), followed by work enclaves (14.4%), mobile work crews (5.3%), and small business enterprises (0.1%) (Revell et al., 1994).

253

- The success of supported employment depends in large part on *job development*, the identification and creation of community-based employment opportunities for individuals with disabilities.
- Although measures such as the number of persons placed, hours worked, wages earned, and taxes paid are important outcomes in evaluating supported employment programs, so, too, is job satisfaction. When 34 supported employees were interviewed (22 who were in individual placements and 12 in the workstation model), the majority said they (1) liked their jobs, (2) were satisfied with the supports they received from their job coach, (3) had had input into selecting their jobs, (4) would rather work in the community than in a sheltered workshop, and (5) had friends at work (Test, Hinson, Solow, & Keul, 1993).
- Rusch, Johnson, and Hughes (1990) found fairly extensive involvement with nondisabled co-workers by supported employees working in individual or workstation placements regardless of the supported employees' level of disability. Supported employees working in mobile crews, however, experienced far less co-worker involvement.
- A paid co-worker was used to support the employment of two individuals with severe and multiple disabilities as hotel laundry attendants (Hood, Test, Spooner, & Steele, 1996).

- The role of the employment specialist/job coach is evolving from one of primary supporter for the employee with disabilities to one who works with the employer and co-workers to create innovative and natural support networks.
- Self-monitoring, self-evaluation, learning how to respond independently to the cues that occur naturally in the workplace, and self-instructions are four ways that employees with disabilities can increase their independence and job productivity in the workplace.
- Many adults with severe disabilities work in sheltered workshops that provide one or a combination of three kinds of programs: training for competitive employment in the community, extended or long-term employment, and work activities.

<ul><li>Mithaug, Martin, and Agran (1987) describe an approach they call the *adaptability model* designed to help students learn independence in the workplace. Instructional activities are designed to foster four kinds of skills inherent in self-determination; decision making, independent performance, self-evaluation, and making adjustments the next time they perform the task.</li><li>Agran and Moore (1994) provide training scripts and monitoring forms for teaching self-instruction of job skills to students with mental retardation. Additional information on how to increase the independence and problem-solving skills of secondary students with disabilities can be found in Agran (1997) and Wehmeyer, Agran, and Hughes (1998).</li><li>The average wage of all persons with mental retardation who worked in sheltered employment settings in 1987 was $1.02 per hour (Lakin, Hill, Chen, & Stephens, 1989).</li></ul>	<ul><li>Today, an IFC-MR facility serving 16 or more residents is considered an institution.</li><li>A person who has just left an institution needs support in the community. Some former residents of state institutions experience "relocation syndrome" (Cochran, Sran, & Varano, 1977) or "transition shock" (Coffman & Harris, 1980) as a result of being dumped into the community without the necessary skills to cope successfully in their new environment and without easy access to support and follow-up services to see that the transition was successful.</li></ul>
	<ul><li>Deinstitutionalization</li><li>foster home</li><li>apartment cluster</li><li>co-residence apartment</li><li>maximum-independence apartments</li><li>supported living</li></ul>
Residential Alternatives	<ul><li>More community-based residential services mean greater opportunities for adults with severe disabilities to live in more normalized settings.</li><li>Despite deinstitutionalization—movement of persons with mental retardation out of large public institutions and into smaller community-based residences such as group homes—approximately 60,000 persons, mostly adults with severe or profound mental retardation, still live in large institutions.</li></ul>

- More than half of all adults with mental retardation who receive residential services live in community group homes of fewer than six residents (Lakin, Braddock, & Smith, 1996), and the number is growing each year as closure of institutions continues.

- The Home Observation for Measurement of the Environment (HOME) is a 100-item scale that measures various aspects of a home environment and daily care practices of care providers (Bradley & Caldwell, 1979). The Home Quality Rating Scale (HQRS) is an attempt to measure the sense of love and attachment shown by care providers to the person with disabilities in a foster care setting and family participation in providing care (Meyers, Mink, & Nihira, 1981).

- Two studies analyzing real estate transaction data have found that neighborhood property values were not adversely affected by group homes. One study examined the sale prices of 525 homes sold around 13 group homes in and around Omaha, Nebraska (Ryan & Coyne, 1985); a second study analyzed the sale of 388 properties near 19 group homes in the Pittsburgh, Pennsylvania, area (Gelman et al., 1989).

- Apartments and small group homes are the fastest-growing living arrangement for adults with disabilities. One-third of individuals with mental retardation who receive residential support services now live in community residences with one to three persons (Anderson, Lakin, Polioster, & Prouty, 1998).

- Foster home placement allows the adult with disabilities to participate in day-to-day activities of family life, to receive attention from people interested in his development, and to experience close personal relationships.

- Apartment living offers the greatest opportunities for integration into the community and interaction with people without disabilities. Three common forms of apartment living for adults with disabilities are the apartment cluster, the co-residence apartment, and the maximum-independence apartment.

- Supported living is an approach toward helping people with disabilities live in the community as independently and normally as they can by providing a network of various kinds and levels of natural supports.

It is estimated that 85% of persons with mental retardation or developmental delays live with their families or on their own without support from the public residential care system (Amado, Lakin, & Menke, 1990). The cost to society to support families in caring for their adult offspring with disabilities is small compared with the cost of providing public out-of-home residential services (Fujiura, Roccoforst, & Braddock, 1994). These individuals, however, do not experience the same level of independence and self-determination.

- The supports needed by a person with severe disabilities to make an important difference in the quality of her social life at home may be as simple as help with a personal schedule, introductions, and photo activity file with which to indicate preferences (Werner, Horner, & Newton, 1997).

- There are numerous conceptions and definitions of quality of life, debates over how or whether it can be measured, and recommendations of what should or must be done to improve it (e.g., Dennis, Williams, Giangreco, & Cloniger, 1993; Halpern, 1993; Hatton, 1998; Sands & Kozleski, 1994; Schalock & Bogale, 1990; Wehmeyer, 1994).
- Giving students the responsibility of directing and managing their own IEP is an excellent way to help them learn self-determination and independence (Martin & Marshall, 1995).

- handicapism

Recreation and Leisure

- Learning to participate in age-appropriate recreation and leisure activities is necessary for a self-satisfying lifestyle.

The Ultimate Goal: A Better Life

- Adults with disabilities continue to face lack of acceptance as full members of society.
- Handicapism—discriminatory treatment and biased reactions toward someone with a disability—occurs on personal, professional, and societal levels. It must be eliminated before normalization can become a reality for every man and woman with a disability.

- Persons with disabilities have begun to assert their legal rights, challenging the view that persons with disabilities are incapable of speaking for themselves.

- The success of a young adult with Down syndrome is attributed to intensive early intervention, regular home-school communication, inclusive academic and social activities, systematic, direct instruction, opportunities to make choices, and early career education.

Profiles & Perspectives: Sebine: Twelve Years Later—"I Need a Vacation"

CHAPTER FIFTEEN
TRANSITION TO ADULTHOOD

Guided Review

I. How Do Former Special Education Students Fare as Adults?
   A. Employment Status
      1. How many adults with disabilities are unemployed?

         a) _____

   B. Wages and Benefits
      1. What is the average income of individuals with disabilities?

         a) _____

   C. Postsecondary Education
      1. What percentage of people with disabilities have taken at least one postsecondary course?

         a) _____

      2. What percentage of people with disabilities are enrolled in postsecondary programs within three to five years of leaving high school?

         a) _____

   D. Dropouts
      1. What percentage of people with disabilities dropped out of school?

         a) _____

   E. Living Arrangements and Community Participation
      1. What percentage of people with disabilities live independently after being out of high school for five years?

         a) _____

   F. Overall Adjustment and Success
      1. The NTLS includes a measure of adult adjustment that assesses independent functioning in what three domains?

         a) _____

         b) _____

         c) _____

2. What percentage of youth with disabilities met these three criteria after being out of school for two years?

   a) _____

3. What percentage of people with disabilities met these criteria after being out of school three to five years?

   a) _____

II. Transition from School to Adult Life: Models and Services
   A. What are the three levels of Will's bridges model of school-to-work transition?

      1. _____

      2. _____

      3. _____

   B. What domains does Halpern's three-dimensional model address?

      1. _____

      2. _____

      3. _____

   C. How does IDEA define transition services?

      1. _____

      2. _____

      3. _____

   D. Individualized Transition Plan
      1. What are the key points to remember when developing ITP plans?

         a) _____

         b) _____

            _____

         c) _____

         d) _____

            _____

         e) _____

            _____

III. Employment
    A. Competitive Employment
        1. A person who is competitively employed:

            a) _____

            b) _____

            c) _____

        2. What are three characteristics of good secondary school programs?

            a) _____

            b) _____

            c) _____

    B. Supported Employment
        1. What is supported employment?

            a) _____

            b) _____

            c) _____

            d) _____

            e) _____

        2. What are the four types of supported employment?

            a) _____

            b) _____

            c) _____

            d) _____

        3. What are the four components of the individual placement model?

            a) _____

            b) _____

            c) _____

            d) _____

4. What is the enclave model?

    a) _____

    _____

5. What is the mobile work crew model?

    a) _____

    _____

6. What is the small business enterprise model?

    a) _____

C. Learning Independence and Adaptability on the Job
1. What are three categories of measures used to evaluate the performance of people with disabilities?

    a) _____

    b) _____

    c) _____

2. What are the drawbacks of outside assistance?

    a) _____

    b) _____

    c) _____

    d) _____

    e) _____

    f) _____

3. What are natural supports?

    a) _____

    _____

4. The importance of co-workers
    a) What four-step procedure can co-workers use (Curl, 1990)?

        1) _____

        2) _____

3) _____

4) _____

5. Self-management
   a) What two self-management behaviors can increase job productivity?

      1) _____

      2) _____

   b) What four statements are used in a self-instructional procedure (Hughes & Rusch, 1989)?

      1) _____

      2) _____

      3) _____

      4) _____

D. Sheltered Employment
   1. What are three types of programs offered in sheltered workshops?

      a) _____

      b) _____

      c) _____

   2. What are three types of business ventures in sheltered employment?

      a) _____

      b) _____

      c) _____

   3. What are the problems with sheltered workshops?

      a) _____

      b) _____

      c) _____

      d) _____

IV. Residential Alternatives
   A. Institutions
      1. What is deinstitutionalization?

         a) _____

B. Group Homes
   1.   What are two key aspects of group homes that make them a more normalized place to live?

      a) _____

      b) _____

C. Foster Homes
   1.   What are the advantages of foster homes for people with disabilities?

      a) _____

      b) _____

      c) _____

D. Apartment Living
   1.   What are three types of apartment living?

      a) _____

      b) _____

      c) _____

E. Supported Living
   1.   What are the nine principles of supported living (Klein, 1994)?

      a) _____

      b) _____

      c) _____

      d) _____

      e) _____

      f) _____

      g) _____

      h) _____

      i) _____

   2.   Supported living, supported employment, and inclusion share what four fundamental philosophical positions?

      a) _____

         _____

b) _____

_____

c) _____

_____

d) _____

_____

V. Recreation and Leisure
   A. Appropriate recreation and leisure activities do not come easily for many adults with disabilities because:

      1. _____

      2. _____

      3. _____

   B. The leisure activities of people with disabilities often include:

      1. _____

      2. _____

      3. _____

   C. What is the crucial element for using leisure time?

      1. _____

VI. The Ultimate Goal: A Better Life
   A. Quality of Life
   B. What are seven forms of handicapism?

      1. _____

      2. _____

      3. _____

      4. _____

      5. _____

      6. _____

      7. _____

C. Self-Advocacy
   1. What does self-determination involve?

      a) _____

      b) _____

      c) _____

      d) _____

      e) _____

D. Still a Long Way to Go
   1. What variables determine a person's quality of life?

      a) _____

      b) _____

CHAPTER FIFTEEN
TRANSITION TO ADULTHOOD

Objectives

1. Summarize the data on how former special education students fare as adults regarding employment, postsecondary education, incarceration, and quality of life.

2. Describe the various models and services for transition from school to adult life.

3. Discuss how secondary school programs can enhance competitive employment prospects for young adults with disabilities.

4. Explain what is meant by *supported employment*.

5. Explain the role of the employment specialist.

6. Describe how self management can be implemented to promote successful employment.

7. Describe the limitations of sheltered workshops.

8. Describe the following types of residential alternatives: group homes, foster homes, and apartment living.

9. Discuss the importance of recreation and leisure in the lives of individuals with disabilities.

10. Explain how handicapism affects the quality of life for individuals with disabilities.

Self-check Quiz

1. What percentage of adults with disabilities are unemployed?
   a. 20%-30%
   b. 35%-50%
   c. 50%-75%
   d. 80%-90%

2. The NTLS found an employment rate of _____ for young adults with multiple disabilities three to five years after secondary school.
   a. 10%
   b. 17%
   c. 25%
   d. 36%

3. Which of the following factors reduce the probability that students with disabilities will drop out of school?
   a. low absenteeism
   b. good grades
   c. socializing with other students outside of school
   d. both a & c

4. Which of the following statements regarding the living arrangements and community involvement of adults with disabilities is true?
   a. About half of adults with disabilities said their disability prevented them from community involvement.
   b. One of every four adults with learning disabilities was satisfied with his/her social life.
   c. More adults with disabilities live independently (alone, with roommate, in dormitory) than dependently.
   d. all of the above

5. Successful transition has been defined by which of the following criteria?
   a. supported employment
   b. independent living
   c. involvement in one leisure activity
   d. both b & c

6. Which is NOT one of the levels in Will's bridges model of school-to-work transition?
   a. outcome-oriented services
   b. ongoing employment service
   c. time-limited transition service
   d. no special transition service

7. At what age must a statement of the child's transition service needs be included in the IEP?
   a. 14
   b. 16
   c. earlier than 16 if deemed appropriate by the IEP team
   d. both b & c

8. When writing an ITP, what are the areas in which outcomes and goals are specified?
   a. employment, residential, social skills
   b. employment, postsecondary education/training, residential, functional skills
   c. employment, postsecondary education/training, residential, recreation/leisure
   d. employment, postsecondary education/training, residential, self-advocacy

9. Systematic coordination between schools and community-based adults services:
   a. has not typically occurred.
   b. has been in place since the passing of PL 94-142 in 1975.
   c. is ultimately the responsibility of the school.
   d. both a & c

10. Why does IDEA (PL 105-17) mandate that a statement of the student's transition service needs be included in an IEP beginning at age 14?
    a. to replace separate transition services a student receives beginning at age 16
    b. to focus attention on curriculum and course planning related to postschool success
    c. both a & b
    d. none of the above

11. Which of the following is a characteristic critical to good secondary special education programs?
    a. The curriculum must stress academic skills.
    b. School-based instruction should be carried out in integrated settings.
    c. Community-based instruction should begin by age 12 for students with severe disabilities.
    d. both b & c

12. Which type of supportive employment is characterized by performance of real paid work in regular, integrated worksites and requires ongoing support from a supported work specialist?
    a. sheltered workshops
    b. mobile work crew
    c. individual placement model
    d. small business enterprise model

13. Which of the following is the most widely used supported employment approach?
    a. sheltered workshops
    b. mobile work crew
    c. individual placement model
    d. small business enterprise model

14. Supported employment is:
    a. competitive work in separate settings for people with disabilities.
    b. for individuals with mild disabilities
    c. for individuals with the most severe disabilities.
    d. both a & b

15. Which of the following residential alternatives offer the greatest opportunities for integration into the community?
    a. apartment living
    b. foster home placement
    c. group homes
    d. residential treatment centers

ANSWER KEYS TO SELF-CHECK QUIZZES

Chapter 1
1. c; 2. b; 3. a; 4. a; 5. b; 6. d; 7. b; 8. d; 9. c; 10. a; 11. d; 12. b; 13. d; 14. c; 15. d

Chapter 2
1. d; 2. a; 3. d; 4. b; 5. c; 6. c; 7. d; 8. b; 9. a; 10. a; 11. d; 12. c; 13. b; 14. b; 15. a

Chapter 3
1. a; 2. d; 3. a; 4. c; 5. d; 6. a; 7. b; 8. d; 9. c; 10. b; 11. d; 12. a; 13. a; 14. c; 15. b

Chapter 4
1. d; 2. b; 3. c; 4. b; 5. c; 6. a; 7. c; 8. b; 9. a; 10. c; 11. a; 12. d; 13. c; 14. b; 15. a

Chapter 5
1. a; 2. d; 3. c; 4. a; 5. b; 6. d; 7. a; 8. a; 9. d; 10. c; 11. b; 12. d; 13. d; 14. b; 15. c

Chapter 6
1. b; 2. d; 3. a; 4. a; 5. d ; 6. a; 7. b; 8. d; 9. a; 10. c; 11. a; 12. a; 13. c; 14. b; 15. a

Chapter 7
1. c; 2. c; 3. d; 4. a; 5. b; 6. c; 7. a; 8. b; 9. d; 10. c; 11. a; 12. c; 13. d; 14. d; 15. b

Chapter 8
1. a; 2. c; 3. d; 4. b; 5. c; 6. b; 7. b; 8. d; 9. a; 10. d; 11. a; 12. c; 13. b; 14. a; 15. c

Chapter 9
1. b; 2. d; 3. a; 4. d; 5. a; 6. d; 7. a; 8. b; 9. c; 10. d; 11. a; 12. d; 13. a; 14. b; 15. c

Chapter 10
1. c; 2. a; 3. a; 4. b; 5. d; 6. c; 7. a; 8. b; 9. c; 10. d; 11. b; 12. a; 13. c; 14. b; 15. b

Chapter 11
1. a; 2. b; 3. d; 4. c; 5. a; 6. c; 7. b; 8. a; 9. b; 10. d; 11. d; 12. d; 13. c; 14. c; 15. c

Chapter 12
1. b; 2. c; 3. a; 4. d; 5. c; 6. d; 7. d; 8. c; 9. b; 10. c; 11. b; 12. a; 13. c; 14. a; 15. d

Chapter 13
1. c; 2. a ; 3. d; 4. b; 5. a; 6. a; 7. d; 8. a; 9. c; 10. b; 11. d; 12. a; 13. a; 14. c; 15. c

Chapter 14
1. d; 2. b; 3. a; 4. b; 5. c; 6. d; 7. b; 8. d; 9. c; 10. a; 11. c; 12. d; 13. c; 14. d; 15. a

Chapter 15
1. c; 2. b; 3. d; 4. a; 5. b; 6. a; 7. a; 8. c; 9. d; 10. b; 11. d; 12. c; 13. c; 14. c; 15. a